Enriching Lives

厚生
利群

Enriching Lives

A History of Insurance in Hong Kong, 1841–2010

Feng Bangyan and Nyaw Mee Kau

Translated by Violet Law

HKFi
The Hong Kong Federation of Insurers
香港保險業聯會

香港大學出版社
HONG KONG UNIVERSITY PRESS

This book is a revised translation of《厚生利群：香港保險史，1841–2008》published in Chinese by the Joint Publishing (HK) Co. Ltd in 2009.

Hong Kong University Press
14/F Hing Wai Centre
7 Tin Wan Praya Road
Aberdeen
Hong Kong
www.hkupress.org

ISBN 978-988-8028-70-2

British Library Cataloguing-in-Publication Data
A catalogue record for this book is available from the British Library.

Designed by Cynthia NG Ying Fai
Printed and bound by Kings Time Printing Press Ltd., Hong Kong, China

Table of Contents

Foreword

by Chan Kin Por, member, Hong Kong Legislative Council
(Functional Constituency — Insurance)

Having grown from a cottage industry covering commercial seafaring ventures to a full-blown diversified and globalized financial centre, Hong Kong's insurance industry has withstood the test of many vicissitudes over the past century.

However, for reasons unbeknownst to most, no completed recorded history existed of this amazing journey. If nothing were done about this vaccuum, valuable historical materials would be obliterated by the passage of time.

This is where the Hong Kong Federation of Insurers has stepped up to the plate.

Enriching Lives: A History of Insurance in Hong Kong, 1841–2010 was born of the urgency to document the evolution and influence of the sector. This rigorous work is an important contribution to the industry.

On behalf of the insurance sector constituency, I thank the authors for their endeavour. I hope the sector will continue to thrive by improving customer service and professional standards.

Foreword

by Allan K. N. Yu, chairman (2010–11), Hong Kong Federation of Insurers

It was my greatest pleasure to have witnessed the fruition of the book project during my tenure as HKFI's chairman.

The writing of *Enriching Lives: A History of Insurance in Hong Kong, 1841–2010* was made possible by the scores of industry veterans who generously contributed their time and thoughts. Their recollection of little known vignettes casts the industry in a humanistic light.

In a sense, the book serves as a compilation of oral history. It is a happy marriage of history and human interest.

Preface

by Peter C. H. Tam, chief executive, Hong Kong Federation of Insurers

This book owes its conception to an idea, plus a bit of kismet.

When I joined the Hong Kong Federation of Insurers in 2004, one of my mandates was to improve the image of the insurance industry, so that more seasoned professionals and young university graduates alike would be inspired to enter the field and the public would put more trust in the practitioners.

I realized very early on all this couldn't possibly be accomplished with hollow slogans or cheap commercials. A more efficacious means is to give the industry flesh and blood by telling the story of how the insurance industry has contributed to Hong Kong's society, economy and the public's well-being.

With that idea in mind, I set about planning for a book project that would trace and explicate the industry's more-than-a-century-long development in depth and in breadth.

Much as I felt encouraged by the enthusiastic backing of the HKFI's governing committee, I was keenly aware this could prove to be an arduous undertaking. To pull it off, it would require, among other things, the right people in the right place.

I didn't know where to start when I visited the University of Hong Kong library system for preliminary research. Only when I browsed the Hong Kong Collection at the Hung On-To Memorial Library on the first floor of the University's Main Library did the eureka moment come. I chanced upon a book called *Chinese Banking in Hong Kong and the Asia Pacific Region* by Professor Mee Kau Nyaw, former vice president of Lingnan University and chair professor of management at The Chinese University of Hong Kong.

Right away I wrote Professor Nyaw to present my idea for a book on a complete, coherent history of Hong Kong's insurance industry. Not only did Professor Nyaw respond quickly and favourably, he also introduced me to his soon-to-be collaborator Professor Feng Bangyan, then dean of the College of Economics of Jinan University in Guangzhou.

The rest, as they say, is history.

The birth of this book, in original Chinese and English translation, became a milestone in its own right on the industry's long winding road of development. It also is a sign of unity of our sector, where all practitioners answered the clarion call for a recorded history.

Enriching Lives is the product of Professors Feng and Nyaw's painstaking research, as well as the insights and wisdom of countless industry leaders and veterans.

For all that, I extend my deepest eternal gratitude.

Acknowledgements

This book was made possible by the contributions of many people. Numerous industry veterans generously gave us their efforts and time. We specifically extend our gratitude to Bernard Charnwut Chan, Chan Kin Por, Johnny Chen, M. K. Cheng, K. P. Cheng, Clement Cheung, Vincent Cheung, H. C. Wong, W. S. Ching, Andrew Chow, K. S. Choi, C. F. Choy, Jackie Chun, K. C. Hong, Y. Ko, Agnes Koon, Kenneth Kwok, Richard Kwok, Sidney Ku, Allan Lam, Alwin Lam, Y. T. Yeung, Anthony Lau, Steven Lau, O. F. Leung, Alvin Li, Mike Lee, Johnson Lee, Geoffrey Lung, Teresa Ma, Y. C. Pi, Michael Somerville, Joe Sun, Edmund Tse, C. C. Wat, James Wong, K. H. Wong, William Woo, George Yan, Andrew Yang, and Allan Yu.

We would also like to thank local institutions within the insurance sector and beyond it for their unstinting support of this project. These are the Actuarial Society of Hong Kong, the Chinese Insurance Association of Hong Kong, the Chinese Underwriters Club, the Employees' Compensation Insurance Residual Scheme Bureau, the Hong Kong Insurers' Club, the Hong Kong Chamber of Insurance Intermediaries, the Hong Kong Confederation of Insurance Brokers, the Hong Kong Export Credit Insurance Corporation, the Hong Kong Federation of Insurers, the Hong Kong General Insurance Agents Association, the Hong Kong Insurance Practitioners General Union, the Hong Kong Society of Certified Insurance Practitioners, the Hong Kong University Library, the Institute of Financial Planners of Hong Kong, the Insurance Claims Complaints Bureau, the Insurance Institute of Hong Kong, the Life Underwriters Association of Hong Kong, the LOMA Society of Hong Kong, the Motor Insurers' Bureau of Hong Kong, the Office of the Commissioner of Insurance of Hong Kong SAR, the Professional Insurance Brokers Association, and The General Agents and Managers Association of Hong Kong.

The contributions of leading insurers, many of which have played a critical role in the historical development of the insurance sector in Hong Kong, have also been instrumental. The American International Assurance Co. Ltd., American International Assurance Co. (Bermuda) Ltd., the AXA China Region Insurance Co. (Bermuda) Ltd., the BOC Group Life Assurance Co. Ltd., the China International Holdings Co. Ltd. (now Taiping

Insurance Holdings Co. Ltd.), the China International Reinsurance Co. Ltd. (now Taiping Reinsurance Co. Ltd.), the Dah Sing Life Assurance Co. Ltd., the Hang Seng Insurance Co. Ltd., HSBC Insurance (Asia) Ltd., Manulife (International) Ltd., MSIG Insurance (Hong Kong) Ltd, the Hong Kong Branch of the Munich Reinsurance Co., the former Pacific Century Insurance (now Fortis Insurance Asia), the Prudential Assurance Co. Ltd., Sun Life Hong Kong Ltd., The Ming An (Holdings) Co. Ltd., The Ming An Insurance Co. (H.K.) Ltd. (now China Taiping Insurance (HK) Co. Ltd.), Transamerica Life (Bermuda) Ltd., and the Zurich Insurance Group (Hong Kong): We offer all of these companies our heartfelt thanks.

Last but hardly least, this book was conceived thanks to the tireless efforts of certain key staff members of the Hong Kong Federation of Insurers. These were Chief Executive Peter Tam, Deputy General Manager, Corporate Communications Selina Lau and Manager – Corporate Communications Cristal Tam. The Chinese and English versions benefited, respectively, from the editorial acumen of Anne Lee, deputy editor-in-chief of the Joint Publishing (HK) Co. Ltd., and Michael Duckworth, publisher of Hong Kong University Press.

Introduction

Insurance is one of the oldest industries in Hong Kong, and it has long played a significant role in the city's economic development. Suffice it to say that the insurance industry has evolved in step with the economy at large. In essence, the industry's development encapsulates that of the overall development of the territory.

The industry's birth in Hong Kong can be traced to the establishment of the Canton Insurance Office Ltd. and the Union Insurance Society of Canton in the nineteenth century. Canton Insurance was jointly formed, and run, by turns, by Davidson-Dent (later called Dent & Co.) and Magniac & Co. (forerunner of Jardine, Matheson & Co.). In 1835, Dent quit the joint operation and set up Union Insurance. The following year, Jardine re-established Canton Insurance as a limited liability company.

After the British took over Hong Kong in 1841, Canton Insurance and Union Insurance moved their bases of operations and registered for business in what was soon to be the Crown colony. This made them the territory's earliest insurers. The subsequent development of the insurance industry in Hong Kong can be broken down into five phases, chronologically:

- The first phase runs from 1841 until the start of the Japanese occupation in 1941. This phase marks the industry's fledgling days. In the 1860s, riding on its superior geographical advantages, Hong Kong took off as a newly opened free trade port. The concentration of foreign firms in the colony laid the foundation for the rise of shipping and international trade. Early on, the economy showed its promise of prosperity.

During this period, insurance, much like banking and shipping, became an important department in most foreign firms; investing in an insurance arm was all the rage among them. By the early 1940s, there were about 100 insurers in the colony. Nearly all were British-controlled subsidiaries that acted as agents and offered a single line of products related to shipping and trading; they primarily served foreign traders.

- Phase 2 runs from the end of World War II until the late 1960s, marking a transition within the industry. The 1950s and 1960s saw Hong Kong evolving from an entrepôt into the light-manufacturing hub of the Far East. As the economic base evolved, so did the insurance industry. Although marine products saw further growth, the competition became more cut-throat than ever. Fire products were thriving, while accident products, especially auto and employees' compensation, were beginning to grow. In other words, the postwar insurance sector was gradually diversifying.

However, even until the end of the 1960s, the market remained dominated by British insurers, with only a few foreign-funded agencies, locally registered limited liability companies, and subsidiaries of large foreign insurers getting slices of the growing pie.

- The third phase goes from late 1960s until the early 1980s, the period of the industry's globalization and diversification. In the 1970s, with the rise of the stock exchange and continued economic growth, international financial institutions flocked to the city. These favourable macroeconomic developments gave rise to many more upstarts. Not only did foreign insurance firms begin to set up shops, but trading firms, real estate developers, and banks also entered the fray with their own insurance operations.

In addition, the sector began to diversify in scale; small and medium-sized local firms and large international underwriters intensified the competition. By this time, Hong Kong had already established itself as an insurance centre in the Asia-Pacific region.

- Phase 4 is bracketed by the 1980s and the return of Hong Kong to Chinese sovereignty in 1997. In an effort to build Hong Kong into an insurance centre worldwide and to protect investors' interests, the government issued the Insurance Companies Ordinance. This required the establishment of the Hong Kong Federation of Insurers, or HKFI, in August 1988. Under growing pressure in the 1990s from government regulators and the public, the HKFI pro-actively promoted self-regulatory measures, such as managing intermediaries and introducing legal sanctions, and cemented the institutionalization of the industry.

However, as more manufacturers relocated their operations to the Chinese Mainland, the demand for fire and employees' insurance slackened, while that for life products began to dominate the market. This motivated the industry to offer new products and broaden the scope of service to satisfy growing demand for quantity and quality.

- The last phase in the industry's development encompasses the post-handover years until the present. Although by 1997 the number of licensed insurers per capita in Hong Kong was already among the world's highest, the growth in life and bank insurance galloped on. The lucrative margins on life products and the tremendous room for growth set the stage for further development for global concerns and local firms alike.

After weathering the Asian financial crisis of 1997, large and mid-sized banks, tapping their expertise and customer pools, began to enter the life market, either through their own insurance subsidiaries or in joint ventures. For many banks, insurance has become their most important non-interest-generating business. Brokers act as financial advisers to clients. The increasingly competitive marketplace has become one in which it is the very fittest who survive.

Chapter 1
Pioneer Insurers in the New Crown Colony: Canton and Union

> **There can be no form of commercial activity that so clearly reflects the state of trade as that of insurance. No business thrives better on a free flow of international trade.**
>
> — Sir William Shenton, in 1935,
> at the centennial celebrations of the Union Insurance Society of Canton

Sir William's words have stood the test of time. Writing fifty years later, an insurance executive considered them again in a book called *Adventures and Perils: The First Hundred and Fifty Years of Union Insurance Society of Canton, Ltd.*[1] 'That speaker [Sir William] knew then, as we know today, that trade is not simply a matter of two parties agreeing to an exchange of goods or services for good consideration,' Alan Chalkley wrote. 'The conditions under which the exchange takes place, and the value of consideration, are affected by various external factors unrelated to the trade. It can be said that the development of insurance companies like Union reflects the history of their time and place.'

Insurance—one of the oldest industries of the modern world—can trace its origins to the fourteenth century. The earliest incarnation of what we know today as the insurance industry emerged in the Mediterranean cities of Palermo and Genoa, both in what is now Italy.

On 23 October 1347, a business executive named Georgius Lecavellum entered into an agreement with the Genoan owner of *Santa Clara*, a commercial vessel, to bear all potential risks associated with a voyage from Genoa to Majorca. The signed agreement remains the oldest insurance contract ever discovered and is preserved in the national library in Genoa.

Since the fifteenth century, with trade expanding throughout the known world, the insurance industry extended its reach from Italy through Portugal and Spain, to the Netherlands, England, Germany, and the rest of the world.

The first product line was marine insurance, which offered financial coverage for total or partial loss at sea. These products were intricately linked to the development of overseas shipping and foreign trade. The growth of marine insurance was integral to the shipping and foreign trade sectors: it not only exerted significant influence on both but was also constrained by the development of both.

In England, the earliest marine insurance industry to take off was a joint venture between London's merchants and their brokers. As foreign trade thrived in the 1540s, marine insurance had been growing apace in England, so much so that the amount on an insurance contract was widely accepted as the basis on which to calculate the costs of intangible services, such as shipping costs.[2]

At the time, Lombard Street, on the bank of River Thames, became known as the hub of marine insurance activities because of the concentration of Italian insurers there. In 1720, both the Royal Exchange Assurance Corporation and the London Assurance Corporation attained the Crown's seal of approval to operate in marine insurance; at one point they created a duopoly in the market.

However, the duopoly did little to dampen the rise of the individual underwriters. Since the 1690s, the Edward Lloyd Coffee House on Lombard Street had evolved into an information hub for traders, brokers, shipowners, underwriters and others in the industry. In essence, it was the forerunner of the Corporation of Lloyd's. In 1871, after Parliament passed Lloyd's Act, which established insurance industry's legal standing, the corporation

Fig. 1.1
Lombard Street on the River Thames in London, 1830s. The street became known as the hub of marine insurance activities as Italian insurers concentrated their offices there.

formally registered with the government to become the centre of the marine insurance sector in England.

From the eighteenth century onward, the industry grew rapidly throughout England, with London as its centre and with London firms present at all of the country's ports. As the Industrial Revolution came to a close at the end of the eighteenth century, the reach of the insurance industry, in tandem with the expansion of the economy and trade, began to

Fig. 1.2
Guangzhou (Canton) in 1837, the only free trade port in the late Qing Dynasty.

stretch beyond London to other parts of the world—including, in the Far East, Hong Kong and the Chinese Mainland.

The Insurance Industry in China during the Nineteenth Century

In the early nineteenth century, although England emerged as the world's mightiest nation in economic terms, it still sustained a trade deficit with China. From 1781 to 1793, England exported products such as textiles, woven goods, and metalware. Although its exports were valued at as much as 16.9 million taels of silver, they amounted to only about one-sixth of the value of tea imported into England from China.

Foreign trade powers, headed by England, were anxious to crack open China's market—by selling opium. Using Guangzhou (Canton) as their base, American and English business executives affiliated with the British East India Company launched into opium trade and widespread smuggling activities. From 1821 to 1839, the first eighteen years of Emperor Daoguang's reign (Wade-Giles: Tao Kuang), opium shipped to China mushroomed from 4,000 odd chests to more than 40,000, each weighing about 100 to 120 catties, or 50 to 60 kg.

Before the Opium Wars, with the Qing government's closed-door policy and trade restrictions firmly in place, Guangzhou was the only free port on the Mainland. According to *History of Insurance Industry in China*, on the northern bank of the Pearl River, roughly half a mile outside the southwest corner of Guangdong and not far from Huaiyuan station was Thirteen Hong Street, where foreign ships from Europe and elsewhere came to trade, receive cargo and pay levies.

At that time, foreigners trading in China faced the menaces of piracy and war, as well as other unforeseeable risks at sea, so they turned to insurers for financial safeguards. The demand for insurance grew as a result.

'When Western merchants came to China they had, therefore, to provide themselves with insurance facilities as with most other services ancillary to merchanting,' according an analysis of that era.[3] In 1801, a group of foreign merchants in Guangzhou formed a temporary insurance association to cover the value of cargo on each of the members' ship up to 12,000 taels of silver. This marked the entry of foreign insurers into China. A few insurance firms from Calcutta followed suit and set up shop in Guangzhou.

In 1805, the British East India Company's director, W. S. Davidson, founded the Canton Insurance Society, the first English-owned insurer in China, with two English trading firms: Davidson-Dent House, the forerunner of Dent & Co., and Magniac & Company, which became Jardine, Matheson & Co. By 1835, Davidson-Dent bowed out of the partnership to form the Union Insurance Society of Canton on its own. In the era prior to the Opium Wars, Canton Insurance and Union Insurance were the only foreign insurers in China.

Because of the distance and time involved in doing business in China then, foreign insurers found it difficult to handle day-to-day operations and had to entrust management responsibilities to the foreign trading firms.

According to reports published in the *Canton Register* in February 1829, Magniac & Co. acted as agent for six insurers, and Davidson-Dent for four.[4] In 1836, Jardine Matheson found that 'its chief interest, and largest investment, continued to rest in the Canton Insurance Office'. Even so, the firm 'acted as agent for as many as eight companies'.[5]

In 1842, the Chinese and the British concluded the Opium Wars with the Treaty of Nanking, turning Hong Kong over to the Crown and opening five ports to free trade: Guangzhou, Xiamen, Fuzhou, Ningbo, and Shanghai. Of these ports, Shanghai grew the fastest. In the late 1840s, Shanghai leapfrogged Guangzhou and rose as China's main trading hub. Even the Guangzhou-based foreign firms were putting down stakes in Shanghai. By the middle of the nineteenth century, more than 160 foreign firms had established a presence in the city.

As trade grew, so did the risks related to warfare, piracy, and marine mishaps—and thus the unequivocal significance of insurance. As *The Times* of London reported at this time: 'Our merchants are entering [China] as if it were a virgin country; and the first comers here found fortune at their feet. More money, it is said, has been made in China during the last five years than all the years of the East India Company's monopoly . . . "Can you insure?" soon became the anxious inquiry of the Chinese consigners, and the trade of one-third of mankind also lay at the feet of the new adventurers.'[6]

Between the late 1850s and the 1860s, various foreign firms invested in their insurance operations in Shanghai and other ports. For instance, Augustine Heard & Co. was set up in 1859 by a group of American business executives as an agent but used Jardine Matheson and Dent as their agents. Two years later, Heard partnered with three New York City insurers to solicit business from American firms in China on a large scale. This pitched them against the British in the fight for marine insurance market share in China.

In 1862, the American-owned Russell & Co. raised 1 million taels of silver at the time, to fund a new shipping enterprise, the Shanghai Steam Navigation Co., with an insurance subsidiary, the Yangtze Insurance Association. With 200,000 taels in seed money and a singular focus on shipping insurance, Yangtze was set up to dominate the market of its namesake river.

By 1863, five foreign firms, including Gilman & Co., Rathbone, Birley & Co., and Sassoon, Sons & Co., had established an insurance consortium in Shanghai called the North China Insurance Co. Ltd. 'As recently as 15 years ago, there was only one insurance firm: Canton,' *Commercial Reports* noted in 1875. 'Its success no doubt spurred on the establishment of six other firms in less than a decade. The capital of all these firms added up to about £570,000, an equivalent of 2 million taels of silver.' These firms include Canton, Union, and Yangtze, as well as the China Traders' Insurance Co. and the China and Japan Marine Insurance Co.

Fig. 1.3
The Shanghai headquarters of the British-owned North China Insurance Co. Ltd., 1850s.

Following in the footsteps of the global insurance industry, the insurance sector in China also saw its beginnings in marine products.

In 1866, Jardine Matheson founded the first fire insurer in China, the Hong Kong Fire Insurance Co. Business was booming, with margins soaring by as much as 50% and the stock price rising by 400% in its first few years of operations. By the late nineteenth century, few Shanghai insurers were offering fire insurance directly, except for the more prominent insurers such as Union and the North China Insurance Co.; most others acted only as agents. And fire coverage was confined to businesses and residents in the city's International Concession. Insurers would hang a copper or iron medallion over the covered shop or house for ease of inspection and as a marker for fire rescuers. Nearly all clients regarded the medallion as a badge of honour because only the most trustworthy would be accepted for coverage.

Life insurance surfaced in China roughly three or four decades after marine products. In 1846, the British-owned Standard Life Assurance Co. set up shop in southern China, but its clients were nearly all Westerners, and operations remained very small. In 1853, Thomas Moncreiff took the helm of Standard Life in Shanghai. By 1889, Standard Life had devised the first mortality table for the Chinese from 1846 to 1900. In 1897, the British established the China Mutual Life Assurance Co. in Shanghai with an issue of 5,000 shares, raising half a million taels of silver. By 1924, China Mutual had merged with Canada's Sun Life Insurance Co.

The early development of the insurance industry in China caught on at major ports around the country. When Canton Insurance opened for business in Guangzhou in 1805, it created a considerable stir and spurred profiteering locals into action. In 1824, an

Fig. 1.4
The Shanghai headquarters of the British-owned China Mutual Life Assurance Co., 1850s.

affluent merchant from Guangdong established the Zhang Baoshun Co. in Guangzhou, which offered insurance services. The merchant was said to 'have a smart hand and wisdom in trading to have founded an insurance outfit to cover other merchants' goods. This way he insured them against potential losses', according to the earliest written record of Chinese involvement in the insurance industry. But since little is known about Zhang Baoshun, its place as China's first locally owned insurance concern cannot be substantiated.

Based on extant historical records, the first documented Chinese-run insurance enterprise was founded on 25 May 1865 as a subsidiary of a prominent south China firm, De Shing Hao. Known as the Shanghai Yi He Insurance Co., it was a small outfit that insured cargo but not entire vessels. It pioneered the use of bilingual (Chinese-English) insurance contracts and broke foreigners' lock on the domestic insurance market.

The landmark development in the homegrown insurance industry came when Li Hongzhang (Wade-Giles: Li Hung-chang), a leading figure in the Self–Strengthening Movement, founded the China Insurance Merchants' Bureau, and later an insurance offshoot, the Yen Chi He Co. In 1872, Li went on to found the China Merchants' Steam Navigation Co. in Shanghai and buy the *Eton* and two other vessels from Britain. Ironically, Li's fledgling

Fig. 1.5
Li Hongzhang, a leading figure in China's Self-Strengthening Movement, 1870s.

enterprises faced discrimination on their home turf. For instance, when the *Eton* was refused coverage by certain foreign insurers in Shanghai, she was insured by Jardine Matheson and another firm, each charging an exorbitant premium of 15,000 taels of silver for a mere fifteen days' coverage.

Given the foreign insurers' cold shoulder, the merchant company realized it was imperative for Chinese traders to be self-reliant and set up their own shop. In February 1875, Li tasked company directors Tang Tingshu (Tong King-sing) and Hsu Jun with establishing China's first shipping insurance enterprise. By 28 December of the same year, the China Insurance Merchants' Bureau formally opened its doors with broad support from local traders. Their support boosted registered capital amount from the initial 150,000 taels to 200,000 taels, thereby increasing its ability to indemnify.

Even so, the insurance bureau was limited by its financial resources to cover only vessels valued at less than 10,000 taels and cargo at less than 30,000. Most vessels then were already valued at more than 100,000 taels. To indemnify entire vessels, it still would require the involvement of foreign insurers. But foreign insurers would only insure up to 60% of total value, so the remainder was still up to the bureau, thereby compounding risks. Tang and Hsu then raised 250,000 taels more to found the Yen He Marine Insurance Co. in July 1876; the bureau oversaw both the business operation and the books.

By April 1878, the steam navigation company again raised 200,000 taels through a share issue, and it set up the Ji He Shipping Insurance Bureau. When 300,000 taels more were raised, Ji He expanded its offerings to include fire products. In 1886, Yen He and Ji He merged to form the Yen Ji He Marine & Fire Insurance Co. with a combined registered capital of 1 million taels.

Outside the trade development bureau network, other Chinese-owned insurance concerns in those early years included the On Tai Insurance Co. (1877), the Shan On Insurance Co. (1880), the Shanghai Fire Insurance Co. (1882), the Man On Insurance Co. (1882), and the Fook On Marine & Fire Insurance Co. (1894). With the exception of Man On and Fook On, the rest were poorly run and quickly shut down. At the time, most local merchants relied on foreign insurers for re-insurance, and the British-owned Sun Fire Insurance Office Ltd. had nearly the entire re-insurance market to itself.

By 1911, just before the fall of the Qing Dynasty, China had roughly thirty-five locally owned insurers, of which twenty-seven offered marine and fire products and eight did life products. All of them together accounted for no more 10% of the market.

By the mid-eighteenth century, the concept of insurance had found its way into the Chinese' public consciousness. Different translations of the term 'insurance' appeared in business publications and dictionaries.

Hong Kong's First Insurer: The Canton Insurance Society

By the end of the 1830s, a social crisis had emerged in China, prompted by the opium trade and the smuggling activities of the British East India Co. and other British 'free agents'. The call for banning opium grew ever more vociferous. The Qing government dispatched Lin Zexu to Guangzhou to stamp out drug traffic. Lin demanded that all foreign traders in Guangdong Province sign an agreement that they would not deal in opium. Should they violate the agreement, their vessels and all cargo would be confiscated and all involved would be executed.

All foreign traders consented to sign, but Britain's chief superintendent of trade in China, Sir Charles Elliot, rejected the agreement. He ordered all British traders to evacuate to Macau. In June 1839, Lin destroyed all opium stocks in Bocca Tigris (or Humen), striking fear into the dealers' hearts.

Fig. 1.6
Hong Kong's Central district in 1857. Insurance, shipping, and foreign trade would become pillars of the new colony's economy.

A year later, in the name of defending their opium-trading interests, the British invaded China. Sir Charles Elliot, along with a young naval captain named George Elliot, commanded troops from India and, on 25 January 1841, occupied Hong Kong Island. On 7 June, Sir Charles Elliot announced that the island was a free port and allowed vessels to travel back and forth. Hong Kong was thus opened up for business.

On 29 August 1842, Britain and China signed the Treaty of Nanking, making Hong Kong a British colony. With naval protection firmly in place, British companies that had

close associations with opium dealings in Guangzhou and Macau, such as Dent and Jardine Matheson, relocated to the new Crown colony. Their insurance subsidiaries, Canton Insurance and Union Insurance, became the first to locate their headquarters in the territory.

In Hong Kong's insurance industry, the Canton Insurance Society was a pioneer. It was jointly owned by traders in Guangzhou, Calcutta, and Bombay but was run, by turns, by management from the two founding firms, Davidson-Dent and Magniac & Co. Every three years (or, some say, every five), one firm's managers would pass the baton to the other's. Later, Davidson-Dent restructured in Guangzhou as Dent & Co., while in 1832 British merchants William Jardine and James Matheson founded Jardine, Matheson & Co. in place of Magniac. From 1832 on, Canton Insurance was run by Dent and Jardine Matheson, until this joint operating arrangement was terminated in 1835.

Canton's main clients were foreign firms dealing in China, and opium was their most significant stock in trade. Thanks to Canton Insurance, these firms could get coverage within China and claim damages, thereby receiving some measure of protection for their drug trafficking. For example, in the spring of 1834, Jardine Matheson's 488-ton vessel, *Sarah*, set sail from Guangzhou to London, ferrying raw silk, silk goods, rhubarb roots, cinnamon bark, native Chinese vegetables, and sundry goods valued at more than 4 million taels of silver. Her insurance contract was issued by Canton Insurance in Guangzhou.

Canton was dissolved when Dent bowed out of the joint operating agreement in 1835. The next year Jardine Matheson founded the Canton Insurance Office Ltd. When the former Canton Insurance opened for business in Shanghai in the 1830s, the risks associated with sailing the high seas of China and India beggar our imagination today. Ruthless pirates prowled the waters. In 1836, Jardine Matheson resorted to arming itself with a high-speed battleship, the *Falcon*, a 351-ton vessel fitted with square sails and three rudders—the equivalent of a twenty-five-gun cruiser. This ship also took part in the Battle of Navarino.[7]

Figs. 1.7 & 1.8
Jardine, Matheson & Co.'s founders, William Jardine (left) and James Matheson (right).

According to the ship's commander, the *Falcon* could effectively deter and defend against pirates. Jardine Matheson also had outfitted a fleet of high-speed crafts to facilitate the on-time delivery of information, rendering the firm extremely competitive in the trade and insurance arenas.

Canton Insurance often complimented the captains of these vessels for their bravery in fighting piracy. Captain Williams of the *Lady Grant*, for instance, was awarded a silver trophy for his efforts in thwarting pirates in Malaya, when his ship was ferrying newly insured cargo through the Strait of Malacca on 2 February 1836. The trophy was later lost but was eventually bought back from a London auction house. Today, it is exhibited in the halls of the Lombard Insurance Group in London.[8]

After the British took over Hong Kong in 1841, Canton Insurance relocated to Macau and registered there for business. According to *A Brief History of Jardine, Matheson and Company (1832–1932)*, in those early days the company 'appears to have been a private body of underwriters similar to the syndicates of Lloyd's, London, to-day. Prominent firms in Hong-Kong each took one or more shares, and the underwriting was done by Jardine, Matheson & Co. Annually, the syndicate had presented to them in manuscript a report of the year's results, and there seems always to have been something substantial to divide. Indeed, the rates then obtained would make the mouth of an underwriter to-day water freely'.[9]

When agents in India courted the business of opium traders, they touted the shipping services and insurance protection offered by Jardine Matheson. Under Jardine Matheson's management, Canton's reach expanded to London, India, and other far-flung corners of the world.

When Canton Insurance relocated to Hong Kong in 1842, it did not retreat from the mainland market. As soon as China was forced to open up the five treaty ports for business, various Western nations set up concession districts at the port cities and introduced modern infrastructure and trading systems.

Canton Insurance was at the forefront of this rapid growth. In 1848, it opened its office in Shanghai and gradually expanded its coverage to Fuzhou, Tianjin, Shantou, and other cities. Until 1860, Canton Insurance remained the sole insurer in China. It even installed agents in Moscow to serve clients who used the Trans-Siberian railway.

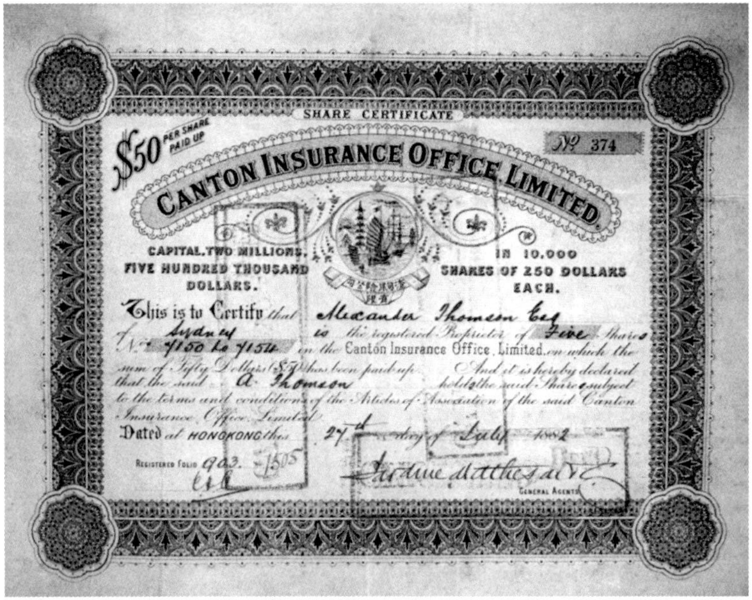

Fig. 1.9
A policy issued by the Canton Insurance Society, a pioneer in Hong Kong's insurance industry.

By 1890, Canton had a presence in more than a dozen Chinese cities, including Xiamen, Guangzhou, Yantai, Fuzhou, Hankou, Jiujiang, Ningbo, Shantou, and Tianjin.[10]

In the latter half of the nineteenth century, Canton Insurance was controlled by a committee of directors populated with a Who's Who of the Hong Kong economic scene, including Hongkong Land's founder, Sir Paul Chater, and chief comprador Sir Robert Ho Tung.[11]

By 1872, Canton Insurance had become a legal entity and adopted a corporate structure to replace the founding partnership. In 1881, the company further restructured itself into a limited liability company, based on the *First Company Ordinance*. Its sizable registered capital of US$2.5 million derived from the issue of 10,000 shares of stock at US$250 each. A few years later, Canton Insurance became one of the founding members of the Institute of London Underwriters.

One of Hong Kong's Earliest Insurers: Union Insurance Society of Canton

Having quit operating Canton Insurance with Jardine Matheson in 1835, Dent & Co. set up the Union Insurance Society in Guangzhou. According to historical records, Dent founded the firm with US$50,000 raised through a stock issue. Jardine Matheson, Turner & Co., and Russell & Co. were among the stakeholders. The firm also welcomed investment from Chinese investors.

Until 1874, Union required stakeholders to share the risks associated with shipping goods to Britain and other parts of the world and to clear all outstanding premiums every three years. This practice was rooted in Union's origins as a mutual assurance society formed by Guangzhou's merchants.[12] These stakeholders-cum-clients raised capital and pooled resources together to cover one another. Even in its fledgling years, Union already had agents in London, Bombay, Calcutta, Singapore, and Manila, reflecting the insurer's early success. When the ports of Hong Kong opened in 1841, Union moved its business operations from Macau and became the first insurer to be headquartered in the new colony.

Fig. 1.10
Pedder Street and the former Bowring Pier in the 1870s. At right, Jardine Matheson's first headquarters; at left, Dent & Co.'s offices and private pier. Canton Insurance and Union Insurance were the two leading insurers when colonial Hong Kong first opened for business.

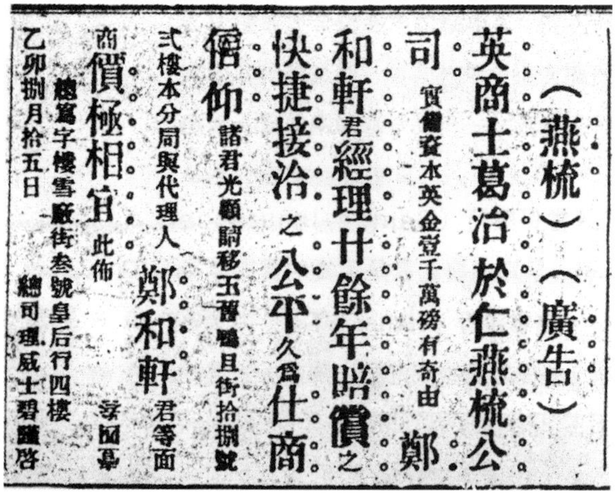

Fig. 1.11
An advertisement for the Union Insurance Society of Canton, late nineteenth century.

The bankruptcy of Dent & Co. in the 1860s was a threat to Union's continued growth. Turmoil in the cotton industry in India in 1866 forced many British firms and banks out of business. Even prominent establishments such as Dent were not spared. When the company declared bankruptcy, Chief Executive Lancelot Dent was replaced by G. D. Williams in 1862. Robert Watmore succeeded Williams in 1868 and served till 1871.

Management personnel changes notwithstanding, Union's business was lifted by the rising tide of Hong Kong's global trade. In 1868, Union installed Samuel Brown as head of its first-ever satellite office, in Shanghai. By 1870, Union's assets mushroomed to US$1.25 million. Each of Union's 250 shares was valued at as much as US$5,000, although shareholders bought in at US$1,000 per share. Major Union stakeholders and directors included Jardine Matheson, Gibb Livingston & Co., Sassoon, Sons & Co., Rathbone, Birley & Co., Ross & Co., Holliday, Wise & Co., Siemssen & Co., and other big foreign firms in Hong Kong.

The ascension of Nathaniel Ede to the top job as secretary of Union in 1871 had a far-reaching impact on Union's future development. During his twenty-six years at the helm, Ede instituted management reforms, laid down new company guidelines, and jettisoned the old convention of triennial accounting. Furthermore, Ede transformed business model from ad hoc, mutual risk-sharing into permanent and unlimited liabilities. Under Ede, however, Union still retained certain features of the old partnership model. For example, Union's new corporate guidelines stated that stakeholders who fail to provide financial support for the firm may have their shares revoked by the board of directors.

Such revoked shares may be re-granted to those who bring businesses to the firm. On 24 October 1882, Union re-registered as a limited liability company under the Hong Kong Corporation Act of 1865 to 1881, with US$1.25 million in assets. Each of the company's 500 shares was valued at US$2,500.

'The change from a short-term society of partners to a permanent corporation denoted not merely a change in legal form,' some commentators pointed out, 'it also betokened a change in the style of management. Shareholders, boards of directors and chairmen might change frequently, but the administrative cadre was perm and stable.

'We see in the Society an early example of the "managerial revolution" which was to affect corporate establishments from that time to the present day. A merchants' mutual had become a corporation with a life of its own. The technocrats, as they were later to be dubbed, were taking over.'[13]

The reforms gave Union a boost, in the form of a broadened scope of business. In January 1874, Union set up a branch in London to compete with better-known and better-funded rival insurers. In 1883, Union opened an office in Melbourne, to expand aggressively its presence in the Oceania market. Union rang in the twentieth century with a flurry of acquisitions. In 1904, it took over Russell & Sturgis, once a Union agent in Manila and a forerunner of Russell & Co., a Union founding stakeholder. Union also bought out the China Traders' Insurance Co. in 1906, the China Fire Insurance Co. in 1916, and the Yangtze Insurance Association in 1925.

Hong Kong's Insurance Industry in the Latter Half of the Nineteenth Century

In its early colonial years, Hong Kong's economic development was at once overshadowed by the opening up of five treaty ports in the Mainland. Although at the time Hong Kong

Fig. 1.12
The paddle steamer *Alaska* was driven aground by the force of a typhoon in Aberdeen, 1874. The ship was typical of the long-haul freighters popular at the time. Marine insurance covering such vessels formed the bulk of the insurance business.

had two established insurers in Canton Insurance and Union Insurance, most policies were still underwritten by big foreign firms. Among them, Jardine Matheson and Dent dominated the market, and most trading firms relied on their underwriting services. In 1844, figures show that of the twenty-five insurers in Hong Kong and Shanghai, eleven were represented by Jardine Matheson and Dent.

In the 1860s, Jardine Matheson even represented the operations of Canton Insurance, Union, the Bombay Insurance Society, the Bengal Insurance Society, the Triton Insurance Co., the Ocean Marine Insurance Co. of Bombay, and two other insurers. At that time, most established trading firms had their own piers, godowns, dockyards, banks—and insurance. Of these units, insurance underwriting vessels and cargo sported healthy margins.[14]

During the 1860s, Hong Kong's growth as a newly opened port was fueled by its natural geographical advantages. A significant presence of foreign firms in the colony already contributed to economic prosperity. In 1867, goods from Hong Kong accounted for 19.8% of the Mainland's total imports, and only 14% of the Mainland's exports went to Hong Kong. Within a decade, these percentages rose to 36.3% and 22.6% respectively.

During Qing Dynasty's waning years, transactions in Hong Kong accounted for at least 30% of China's international trade. As more and more Americans and Europeans traded in China, the demand for insurance services grew apace. Foreign insurers and their agents flocked to the free-trade ports in pursuit of new business opportunities.

Around this time, Chinese-owned banks and insurers began to compete head-to-head with the insurance subsidiaries controlled by big foreign firms, thereby cutting down historically lucrative margins. Meanwhile, using the service of the local Chinese insurers, even small foreign firms could now trade directly on the Mainland. This further eroded the edge big foreign firms had once enjoyed.[15]

Also, the increasing use of freighters in the 1860s, the 1869 opening of the Suez Canal, and the 1871 start of telegram communications between London and the Far East all added to the ease of trading in Hong Kong and other parts of the region.

All this caused the big trading firms to re-evaluate their operations and pay more attention to auxiliary areas critical to foreign trade, such as logistics, underwriting, banking, and port facilities, rather than the mere buying and selling of goods.[16] They recognized that 'insurance and banking grew, like shipping, to be among the firm's most vital functions'.[17]

Against this backdrop, big trading firms in Hong Kong stirred up a frenzy of investment activities in underwriting in the 1860s and 1870s. In 1861, the American-funded Augustine & Heard Co. began to flex its muscle by representing three large American insurers in Hong Kong. Before, Heard would collect commissions but stop short of acting as agents. That summer, the firm emerged as the agent of several large U.S. insurers. This expansion angered its American rival, Russell & Co., because it noticed that the company acted as 'agents for three New York insurance offices . . . offering to take large risks and adjust here, or in England and . . . in India. This indicates a change in the policy of the New York Companies, who not too long ago refused to appoint agents to grant policies'.[18]

In 1862, Russell launched an even more aggressive push than Heard in the underwriting market by establishing the Yangtze Insurance Co. in Shanghai. Registered in Hong Kong with a paid-up capital of 417,880 taels of silver, Yangtze quickly set up branches in London, New York, and Singapore; it also named some thirty agents in mainland ports. Russell acted as agent for Yangtze's clients exclusively to indemnify all of the firm's vessels and cargo. That way, Russell nearly monopolized the shipping insurance market along the Yangtze.

When Russell went out of business in 1891, Yangtze reorganized itself into an independent, British-owned company with a registered capital of 1.2 million taels of silver

and a paid-up capital of 720,000 taels. It rose as one of the major players among foreign insurers in Hong Kong and Shanghai, until its operations were halted in 1941 by Japanese occupying forces.

In 1865, Heard founded and funded the British Traders' Insurance Co. Ltd. (BTIC) in Hong Kong with a registered capital of 2.2 million taels of silver and a paid-up capital of 600,000 taels. BTIC offered fire, marine, and accident insurance products. Its business expanded quickly, and it set up branches in major cities such as Shanghai, Hankou, Tianjin, Guangzhou, Fuzhou, and Beijing, and later in other cities around China and along the Pacific coast. Heard and six other foreign firms, including Russell and Sassoon, pooled an investment capital of 1.5 million taels of silver and set up the Victoria Insurance Co. Heard was in charge of Victoria's day-to-day operations. In 1906, BTIC was taken over by Union Insurance Society of Canton.

Fig. 1.13
The American-funded Yangtze Insurance Co. was established in Shanghai in 1862.

At this time, British firms also stepped up their investments in the insurance market. Even in its early days in the 1850s, the Chinese branches, in Hong Kong and Shanghai, of the Jardine Matheson–controlled Canton Insurance 'prospered; receipts for many months

Fig. 1.14
A blaze in Sheung Wan, c. 1866. Note the absence of fire trucks on the scene.

indicated a larger sale of policies among Chinese than among Western merchants'.[19] To expand Canton's business there, the firm's management began more actively to sell shares to the Chinese. In December 1868, Jardine Matheson's manager in Shanghai, F. B. Johnson, wrote to a Canton Insurance manager: 'I've asked you to allocate more shares to smaller shipping concerns and Chinese firms so as to appease them. If we don't do more to bring these clients into our fold we risk losing our foothold in the Shanghai market. It seems to me that our comprador Tang has done his utmost in currying favor with the Chinese traders. I hope you'd consider using the firm's profits to reward his efforts and cultivate influential local traders.'

By 1866, with the expansion of the scope of coverage, Jardine Matheson established the Hong Kong Fire Insurance Company (HKFIC) in the colony, with a registered capital of HK$2 million and a paid-up capital of HK$400,000. This was the first Hong Kong–based fire insurer the colony had ever seen. Like its European counterparts, HKFIC formed and trained its own fire brigade.[20] A Lombard Co. archivist in London recalled that on Christmas Day 1878 Hong Kong was ravaged by a fierce blaze.

Fanned by strong northeasterly winds, flames licked the area far and wide. Firefighters were forced to demolish lots of surrounding buildings in order to contain the blaze. Residents survived by using wet blankets and rugs to insulate their buildings. Later, a godown packed with loads of firecrackers exploded. Many witnessed the awesome ball of flames looming over the hillside on Hong Kong Island.

In those days, an adjuster called Philip had indelible memories of traditional Chinese pharmacies he had visited on the job. He recalled: 'Surveying these pharmacies was an awful assignment. You ventured down the alleys with the agent. On your way down there you saw jar after jar of pickled awful stuff, such as turtle heads and colorful snakes.

One look at them could make you feel nauseous. And then there were powdered buffalo horns and dried unidentifiable organs of tigers. At first glance, they looked like preserved onions, but they could fetch much higher prices. In evaluating these items for coverage, you needed to keep in mind the tangible value of these "secret ingredients" so that you'd come closer to judging their true worth.'

HKFIC was headquartered in Hong Kong, with branches expanding to Shanghai, Xiamen, Guangzhou, Hankou, Beijing, Shantou, Qingdao, Chongqing, among others. The Shanghai Municipal History Museum has preserved for display an insurance contract issued by HKFIC on 12 June 1924.

The fire insurer saw its business grow at breakneck pace, and margins swelled. Its shareholders made a 50% profit on their initial investment, and stock prices rose by 400%. This was a level of profitability unrivalled by most insurers of the day, thus cementing the company's prominence in the colony. The company also actively expanded its business overseas, including in Japan.

From 1868 to 1870, the insurer stepped up its marketing efforts in Japan. In 1897, it even published a front-page advertisement in the English-language *Japan Times*. But in those heady days the insurer sustained heavy losses in Japan. Seismic activity was frequent, and both Yokohama and Tokyo saw devastating fires, in 1866 and 1892 respectively. Despite this, trade among Japan, Britain, and Hong Kong was by and large smooth-sailing until World War II broke out.

Based on a partial survey, besides BTIC, Victoria, and HKFIC, insurers established in Hong Kong from the 1860s onwards included:

- The Hong Kong Marine Insurance Co, reportedly established in 1862 by the British firm Lindsey & Co., with a branch in Shanghai;

- The China Fire Insurance Co., established in 1864;

- The China Fire Insurance Co. Ltd., established in 1870 with a registered capital of HK$2 million, offered marine, fire, and accident insurance, with Union acting as agent. Although 'China' was part of its name, the firm was in fact owned by British business executives. Headquartered and registered in Hong Kong, it had branch offices in London, Singapore, Bombay, and elsewhere, and agents in Shanghai, Guangzhou, Xiamen, Hankou, Tianjian, Beijing, and Shantou. Industry experts long suspected that the China Fire Insurance Co. and the China Fire Insurance Co. Ltd. were one and the same because of the similarities of their names.[21] With the onset of World War II, the company was ordered to be closed down by the Japanese army;

- The Chinese Insurance Co., established in 1871 by a group of compradors on the Mainland with a registered capital of 1.5 million taels of silver. Because Chinese investors ended up contributing more than half of the 300,000 taels in paid-up capital, the firm was mistaken as a Chinese-owned concern, when in fact it was a joint venture of both Chinese and foreign merchants. Registered in Hong Kong, Chinese Insurance first opened for business in Hong Kong and Shanghai before offering marine coverage at various ports through foreign firm agents such as Dent & Co.;

- The Jardine Insurance Co., established in 1873 as the third insurer under Jardine Matheson. Its prominence was overshadowed by that of the first two;

- The Man On Insurance Co., established in 1891 and headquartered in Hong Kong;

- China Underwriters Ltd., established in 1909 and registered in Hong Kong with expansion into Shanghai.

The latter half of the nineteenth century marked the first peak in the development of Hong Kong's insurance industry with the following noteworthy trends:

(1) Major foreign firms invested in and founded numerous insurers. Headquartered in Hong Kong, these insurers aggressively sought out business in the mainland market. In decades afterwards, this evolved into an insurance business network that covered major cities on the Mainland, with Hong Kong as the nexus. In the early 1870, for instance, Union Insurance already had agents in Shantou, Xiamen, Fuzhou, Ningbo, Shanghai, Zhejiang, Hankou, Yantai, Tianjin, Taiwan, and elsewhere. By 1874, 'Union grew into a great specialized insurance company with worldwide activities', according to the company's written history.[22]

(2) Major foreign firms continued to develop their insurance business via agencies. Although these foreign firms had established their own professional insurance arms, due to the lack of manpower and financial resources and considerations related to the trading environment, they still relied heavily on agents to vie for their share of insurance business in Hong Kong and on the Mainland. Even those insurance firms created by foreign firms were independent in name only and were operated by the firms that had invested in them. To fulfill commissions from important foreign firms, Jardine Matheson made sure to install superior insurance practitioners as managers of branch offices in key areas.[23]

During this time, the foreign firms' agency business underwent significant development. For instance, when Butterfield & Swire Co. Ltd. was established in Shanghai in 1867, it managed to secure agency rights for the big three British insurers in eight years. By 1900, Swire has wrested control of more insurance business in China than any other foreign firm, going head-to-head with Jardine Matheson.

(3) At the time, the development of the insurance industry in Hong Kong was closely associated with foreign firms' dealings in China. While marine products covering vessels and their cargo were the mainstay of these insurers' business, fire products also gradually grew in significance. In 1866, Jardine Matheson founded the Hong Kong Fire Insurance Co., a milestone in this developmental trend. However, the growth of life products lagged far behind. Only in 1898 was the first life contract signed.

Fig. 1.15
A Butterfield & Swire vessel docked in Guangzhou in 1900. Swire already dominated the insurance market in China.

Fig. 1.16
The Wing On Life Insurance Co., one of the most influential Chinese-founded insurers in Hong Kong, was in the building on the right, on the floor under the American flag.

(4) Trade associations for insurers in Hong Kong began to take shape. The first was the Fire Insurance Association (FIA) of Hong Kong, founded in 1895 as a representative organization. In 1903, it was reorganized as a company, with the stated goal to unite practitioners from different parts of the insurance sector doing business on Hong Kong Island, Kowloon, and the New Territories. The purpose of the new trade group was to ensure that every collective action would cover the interest of all member companies. The group was also responsible for drafting regulations governing fire product transactions in all parts of Hong Kong and for providing supervision for all operations. Members were required to have an insurance business in Hong Kong.[23]

Three years later, in 1906, the creation of the Marine Insurance Association (MIA) of Hong Kong followed. Lost records have made it impossible to get a good grasp on the MIA's activities in those early years, but one thing is certain: the two associations forged a close bond from the beginning. The FIA's secretary, A. R. Lowe, also served as the MIA's founding secretary.[24]

Hong Kong's Insurance Industry in the First Half of the Twentieth Century

The insurance industry kicked off the twentieth century at a low point. The civil war in China brought the end of the Qing Dynasty in 1911 and the beginning of prolonged turmoil on the Mainland. Disasters at sea were also rampant. In four short months during 1912 more than forty ships either disappeared or sank, including the *Titanic* on 14 April when more than 1,500 passengers were either killed or injured when it sank. Union paid out £42,000 and the Prudential Assurance Co. Ltd., a British insurer that set up shop in Hong Kong after World War I, £14,000. In addition, warfare on the Mainland cost Union about US$20 million in payouts, exceeding the firm's total assets in 1914.[25]

However, until 1915, Union reported profitable operations in its annual reports and even doled out bonuses to shareholders. With World War I drawing to a close, Union's might

CHEMIS

was boosted, and in 1918 it distributed a £30 dividend and a 20% bonus. In fact, the war had fattened the company's premium revenues from 1.1 million pounds to more than 3 million pounds. Through those years, a singular principle Union hewed close to had been crucial to its success: maintain a high reserve as a safeguard against exigencies.

As one commentator said, 'This conservative philosophy stood it in good stead through many a bad time—not only war and civil violence, storm and flood, fire and destruction, but the fluctuations of currencies and bullion, the wayward imposition of national law and the overthrow of governments.' Although the bonuses never stopped flowing, Union still managed to maintain a high level of reserve capital.[26] 'Times are abnormal,' said Chairman P. H. Holyoak. 'The future is full of uncertainties.'

After World War I, Union expanded its network all over the world. In Asia it had nine branches, including Yokohama and Singapore, as well as Shanghai, Hankou, Beijing, Tianjin, and Guangzhou; in Australia there was Sydney and Melbourne; in North America, its presence included Toronto, Seattle, San Francisco. In Africa, it was Cairo and Johannesburg. With this expansion, Union emerged as a prominent multinational with branches and agents throughout the world.[27]

At the same time, Union's registered capital and total capital were both swelling. In December 1882, Union called a shareholders' meeting to double the face value of each share, to US$5,000, thereby boosting the company's fixed capital to US$250 million, although its paid-up capital remained at US$250,000. In 1916, when Union bought out the China Fire Insurance Co., its fixed capital rose to US$4 million.

As for Union's asset base, it stood at more than US$2 million in 1892 and soared to US$3 million by the end of the century. In 1906, it exceeded US$8.5 million when Union took over the China Traders' Insurance Co. By 1908, it hit the US$10 million mark, and by 1914, assets were valued at US$17 million.

In 1935, at Union's centennial celebrations, Board Chairman S. H. Dodwell brimmed with pride. 'To grow from a small Company brought into existence by a group of merchants in Canton, to a world-wide business owned by shareholders resident in practically every continent, needed foresight and initiative,' he said. 'That this was not lacking in our predecessors is evidenced by our position today. . . . The ability displayed by succeeding underwriters, the successful outcome of their operations and the sound condition of its financial structure have won for the Society a place in [the] London insurance world of which all associated with it have every reason to be proud.'

It was in response to Dodwell's declaration that Union's chairman, Sir William Shenton, made the remark with which this chapter began: 'There can be no form of commercial activity that so clearly reflects the state of trade as that of insurance. No business thrives better on a free flow of international trade.' Sir William then went on: '[C]onsequently, with wars and rumours of wars, prevailing low commodity values, the very small rate of interest earned on capital, the instability of currencies, the gyrations of foreign exchanges, quotas, rising tariffs and the general adoption of almost every form of trade barrier, it is most gratifying to find that the accounts now presented to us are as satisfactory as they are.'[28]

Such was an apt description of Hong Kong's fledgling insurance sector.

In the early years of the twentieth century, various foreign life insurance firms gradually made their way into Hong Kong. Chief among them was Canada's Manufacturers Life Insurance Co. (now called Manulife Financial). Manulife opened for business in Hong Kong and Shanghai in 1897, and by 1898 it established an agency, Bradley & Co. On 23 December 1898, A. H. Ellis, an executive at the agency, sold the first-ever policy for Manulife in southern China. It was a fifteen-year policy for a thirty-one-year-old Chinese man. The policy number was 25042. The coverage was for HK$2,000 at an annual premium of HK$151.61.[29]

Fig. 1.17
The Hong Kong office of the Manufacturers Life Insurance Co. (now Manulife Financial), c. 1935. Manulife had opened for business in the Crown colony in 1897.

At the time, due to a lack of understanding and experience, Manulife's board was sceptical of business prospects in China and even declared at a meeting on 27 June 1900: 'Do not accept business from China without board approval.'

However, they also felt that China was a vast market and worth exploring. So the Toronto headquarters scrutinized its own risk assessment on the region and gradually issued policies through Bradley. At first, Manulife set up its office on Queen's Road Central; it moved to Prince's Building after World War I. In May 1931, Manulife officially opened a southern China branch in Hong Kong and moved its operations to the Hong Kong Club building.

The boundless energy the branch manager showed in promoting life products earned him the chairman's prize in 1932 and pushed the firm's presence into Shantou, Xiamen, and Macau, thus establishing Manulife as the pre-eminent life insurer in Hong Kong and southern China. The other foreign insurer that managed to establish itself in the colony before World War II was the Sun Life Assurance Co. of Canada, which also had an office in Shanghai.

According to surveys, the number of insurance companies, including the sum of their offices, swelled to about a hundred by the early 1940s. At that time the better-funded foreign firms tended to set up only satellite offices in Hong Kong, while Chinese-owned insurers, whose capital tended to be in the tens of thousands of Hong Kong dollars and not much more, based their headquarters in the colony.

Hong Kong's insurance sector was basically buttressed by British firms, which acted as underwriting agents in the course of conducting their shipping and trading businesses. These firms offered mostly products related to those activities and to a clientele comprised primarily of foreign merchants.

Chapter 2
The Establishment and Development of the Chinese-Owned Insurance Sector

> **In the early days, insurance remained an alien import from the West and so foreign insurers ruled the industry ... But a few enlightened local Chinese insurers saw strength in numbers so they banded together to support one another. They weathered through thick and thin and built themselves up.**
>
> — Lo Tai Yiu, Commemorative Booklet of the 80th Anniversary of the Chinese Insurance Association of HK, 1983

Toward the end of the Qing Dynasty, foreign insurers in China began to open up to investments from local merchants. However, Chinese investors were entitled only to profits and not voting rights or any voice in management. In other words, these insurance companies were lopsided joint ventures at best and far from equal partnerships.

The first foreign insurer that solicited Chinese investments was Union Insurance, which, when Dent & Co. founded it in 1830, had a significant capital injection from some Guangzhou business investors. In Shanghai, many foreign enterprises, including insurance companies, also welcomed Chinese money.

In 1868, as recounted in the previous chapter, Jardine Matheson established the Hong Kong Fire Insurance Co. Ltd. It did so in compliance with the colony's newfangled companies ordinance on limited liability companies. At one time, the famous comprador Sir Robert Ho Tung sat on the consulting committee of both Hong Kong Fire and Canton Insurance, another insurance firm controlled by Jardine Matheson.

Based on existing records, the first Chinese-controlled insurance firm was founded by a Shanghai trading firm with close ties to Jardine Matheson. Although that firm covered the

Fig. 2.1
An illustrated promotional calendar by the Fook On Assurance & Godown Co. Ltd.

cargo shipments of Chinese firms and little else, it served to stir up some competition for the foreign insurers.

Chinese-Founded Insurance Companies between the Late Nineteenth Century and the Dawn of the Chinese Republic

The later years of the Qing Dynasty were an incubation period for Chinese-owned insurance companies. The first such enterprise was established in 1877 in Shanghai: the China Traders' Insurance Co. Its founding mission was to keep trading profits within the Chinese business community.

With 1.5 million taels of silver in capital, the company opened up branches not just in Hong Kong but also in mainland cities, offering only marine and fire policies.

In the same year, some prominent Chinese business investors and compradors in Hong Kong pooled $400,000 and set up the On Tai Insurance Co. to cover cargo ships shuttling between Hong Kong and Australia, America, Southeast Asia, and Mainland China. With its Western-style management, On Tai posed a challenge to an insurance and finance industry dominated by foreign insurers. The company joined the Hong Kong General Chamber of Commerce in 1881 and became the first Chinese enterprise to have earned membership in a club long dubbed the 'Western Chamber of Commerce' because its members were predominately American and British traders.

Several other Chinese insurers emerged in Hong Kong during the last decade of the nineteenth century. All, like On Tai, adopted the same word in their names: 'On', which means 'peaceful' in Chinese. All had offices in Shanghai, China's financial centre, as well as other major cities and ports on the Mainland and around Southeast Asia.

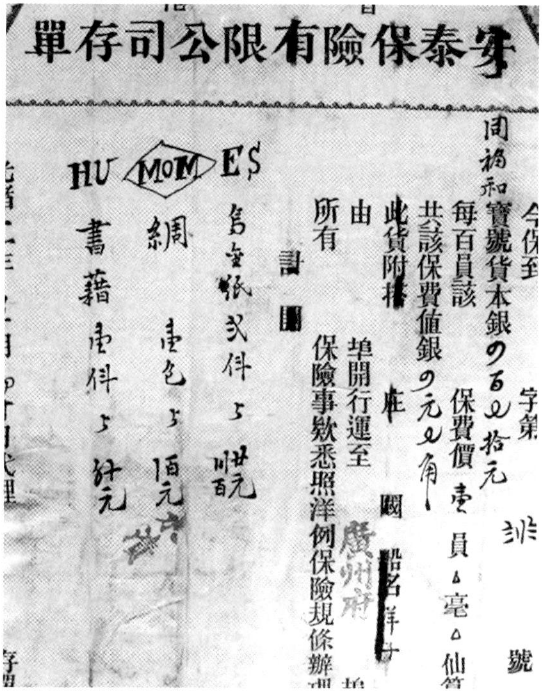

Figs. 2.2 & 2.3
Policies issued by On Tai Insurance, left, and the Tung On Fire Insurance Co. Ltd. right, late 1800s.

All told, from 1865 to 1911, thirty-three Chinese insurers arose in Shanghai, according to the *Shanghai Finance Digest*. By 1937, the count had mushroomed to eighty-seven.

Fig. 2.4 (opposite)
The Shanghai night scene in the 1930s. On the taller spires are the neon signs of Wing On (left) and Sincere (right) department stores.

One of the most noteworthy was Hong On Insurance, co-founded in 1914 by the two most prominent department store chains in Hong Kong: Sincere and Wing On. With a combined investment of $10 million, the insurer offered fire and marine coverage, mortgage-lending services, and other products.

聯益貿易公司
LIENGYI

Fig. 2.5
The Hong Kong Hotel on fire in January 1926.

Fig. 2.6 (opposite)
Connaught Road in Central Hong Kong after a typhoon in 1906.

By 1930, Hong Kong had seen the rise of more than fifty insurers—both local and foreign. Foreign insurers, mostly branches of firms headquartered elsewhere, had far more capital than local firms. The local and foreign firms were at once competitors and collaborators.

Their meagre capital did not allow most local firms to indemnify high-value cargo. So for any coverage worth more than $10 million, local firms had to divide it with foreign firms—

SOUTH CHINA
MORNING POST

usually the better funded among them. The local firms also had to rely on foreign insurers for re-insurance. This inadvertently stymied the growth of local enterprises. The same situation was also evident among Chinese insurers in Shanghai.

When World War II cut off Hong Kong's trade links with England, this risk-sharing practice was no longer possible. Chinese insurers looked to each other to share the risks of a pool of policyholders for the same product line.

K. H. Wong
Executive director and CEO, the Asia Insurance Co. Ltd.
Joined the industry in 1962

I remember back in the 1980s, when foreign brokers just landed here from overseas, they mostly got with international firms and had few dealings with local insurers. At the same time, local Chinese insurers also resisted dealing with foreign brokers who saw only 'gweilos' as business partners. Asia was the first local firm to enter into business partnerships with these foreign brokers.

But when the Chinese-owned insurance firms saw how they've been losing out to these brokers, they got smart and began to forge partnerships. So by the 1990s, nearly all the local guys had joined forces with the foreign brokers, thus resulting in the rapid expansion of international brokerages. Even now, the brokers' position as the intermediary in the insurance market remains rock solid because the majority of clients are under their control.

Chinese Family Insurers: Sincere and Wing On

In the history of the Chinese-owned insurance sector, Sincere and Wing On both exerted a significant influence. Both firms' founders were Chinese-Australian; both got their start in Hong Kong in retail and insurance and found success on the foundation of business diversification.

Figs. 2.7 (below left)
A Sincere advertisement, c. 1910.

Fig. 2.8 (below right)
The Sincere Department Store building on Des Voeux Road in Central as it was from 1917 to 1968.

Sincere's founder, Ying Piu Ma (1864–1944), started his working life as a gold miner in Sydney when he was nineteen. In 1892, Ma, a native of Zhongshan in Guangdong Province, joined a few others from the same area to found a trading firm dealing in sundry Chinese goods and specialties from various cities. He made a fortune. He then moved to Hong Kong and set up new firms to handle imports and exports.

Fig. 2.9
The Ma family, c. 1940. Sincere's founder, Ma Yingpiu, is seated in the centre row, third from right, with his grandchildren.

During his time in Australia, Ma was impressed with the 'no haggling' style of retail operations that prevailed at Western department stores and was determined to introduce such practices in Hong Kong. Once again, he garnered support from his fellow natives. With $25,000, they founded the Sincere Department Store in 1900.[1]

Sincere quickly diversified into other lines of business, including insurance and mortgage lending. In 1915, the Sincere Insurance Co. was established with a registered capital of $1.2 million and paid up at 50%. It offered fire and marine coverage, as well as mortgage-lending services from offices across Guangdong Province and in Tianjin, Shanghai, Singapore, Thailand, and Vietnam. Within a decade, the insurer got a shot in the arm: an additional $600,000 in paid-up capital.

In 1922, the Sincere Life Assurance Co. was founded with $2 million in seed capital from the parent company after consolidation. But almost right away it began to face turmoil that would last for decades, including the labour strife of 1925 in Hong Kong and, later on, the Japanese invasion. As soon as World War II spread to the Pacific, Sincere's branches in Singapore and on the Mainland were forced to suspend operations until the end of the war; only the Hong Kong office managed to carry on, though not without hardships. Finally, the branches in Singapore and Shanghai shut down permanently, in 1948 and 1952 respectively.

Nonetheless, operations in the Hong Kong head office continued to grow steadily and branched out to property investment. The 1968 completion of a new headquarters building in Central laid down a milestone in the development and diversification of Sincere Insurance.

At first, Sincere Life had a hard time cracking the market because most Chinese were strangers to the concept of insurance. However, once Sincere switched gear and promoted life products as a tool to accumulate wealth, this appealed to the savings-

馬南源堂

minded Chinese, and they gradually warmed to the idea. As soon as Sincere got a foothold in the life market once dominated by foreign insurers, four other Chinese-owned life insurers emerged to vie for a piece of the action.

After Sincere, another significant Chinese-owned insurance group, Wing On, also made its first foray into the market. Wing On was founded by the Gock brothers, James Gocklock (1872–1956) and Philip Gockchin (1876–1966), from Guangdong Province. They made

先施人壽保險有限公司

按照香港公司則例組設

THE SINCERE LIFE ASSURANCE COMPANY, LIMITED.

INCORPORATED UNDER THE HONG KONG COMPANIES ORDINANCES
AUTHORISED CAPITAL $2,000,000 IN 200,000 SHARES AT $10 EACH

額定資本二百萬圓分作二十萬股每股十圓

股份票

No. 831 號 SHARE CERTIFICATE Shares 50 股

This is to certify that Mr. Tang Yu Ki of Hong Kong is the registered holder of Fifty shares, numbered 53325 to 53374 inclusive in the above named Company, subject to the Memorandum and Articles of Association thereof, and that upon each of the said shares the full amount of Ten Dollars has been paid up.

Given under the common Seal of the said Company at Hong Kong this Eighteenth day of June One Thousand Nine Hundred and Forty Nine.

The Common Seal of the said Company was hereunto affixed in the presence of

Director

Manager

CANCELLED

茲據
鄧汝基先生遵照本公司註冊章程
附入股份伍拾股由
第五二三二五至五三三七四號
股本每股拾圓計共伍佰圓
經已如數繳足此據
董事 歐炳光
董事
司理
中華民國三十八年六月十八日
先施人壽保險有限公司發給

Fig. 2.10
A stock certificate issued by the Sincere Life Assurance Co. in 1949.

their fortune in Sydney by running a fruit stall, called Wing On, meaning 'perpetual peace' in Chinese.

Seeing how successful Sincere had been as a department store and more, the elder brother, James, dispatched his younger brother to Hong Kong to follow suit. He set up the Wing On Department Store Co. Besides dealing in exports and imports, Wing On also branched out into banking to capture hot money in the market.[2]

Fig. 2.11
Wing On's founding brothers, James Gocklock (left) and Philip Gockchin (right).

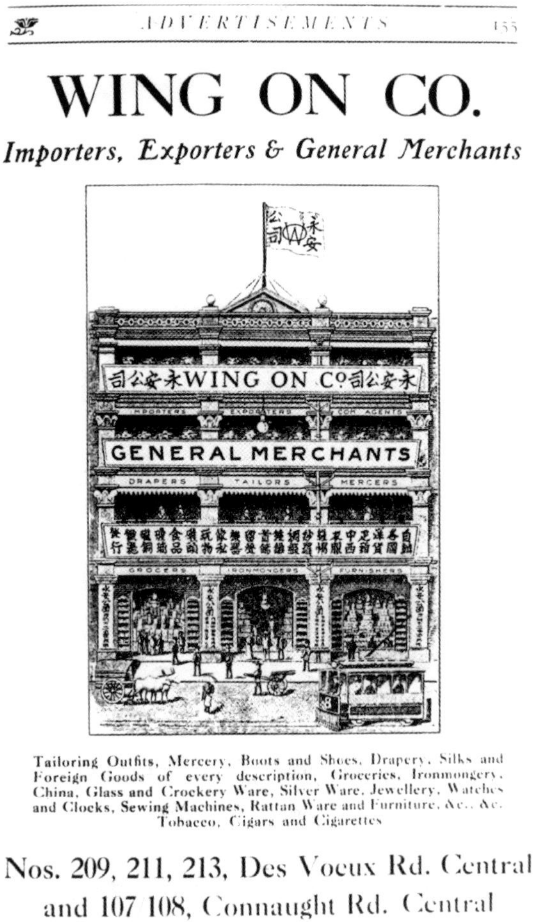

Fig. 2.12
The Wing On Co. building on Des Voeux Road in Central, c. 1910.

James Gocklock arrived in Hong Kong in 1909 and restructured the new firm into a limited liability company. Wing On prided itself on its 'fair trade' principle and was well reputed in business circles. By 1921, the brothers had set up a textiles plant in Shanghai, and a department store followed. Wing On soon expanded into insurance, hospitality, foreign-currency trading, and other sectors, rising as a diversified business enterprise.

In addition to a headquarters in Hong Kong, Wing On opened up branches in Guangzhou, Fuzhou, Yangzhou, and Macau. The brothers' teamwork and effective management of a family business empire quickly earned the family prominence and affluence.

In 1915, the brothers established the Wing On Marine & Fire Insurance Co. Ltd with $750,000. It proved such a hit that clients also demanded life products. So the brothers raised $15 million from local and overseas Chinese and set up the Wing On Life Insurance Co. Wing On's rise was helped by Hong Kong's soaring status as a financial centre in Asia, as well as a growing awareness among customers of the many benefits a life policy could bring. More and more Chinese saw life policy as more than just a savings instrument: it was also financial protection in case of accident. Even though life insurance remained a novel investment tool, this dawning awareness and trust in reputable names such as Wing On served to cement the foundation for the life insurance business.

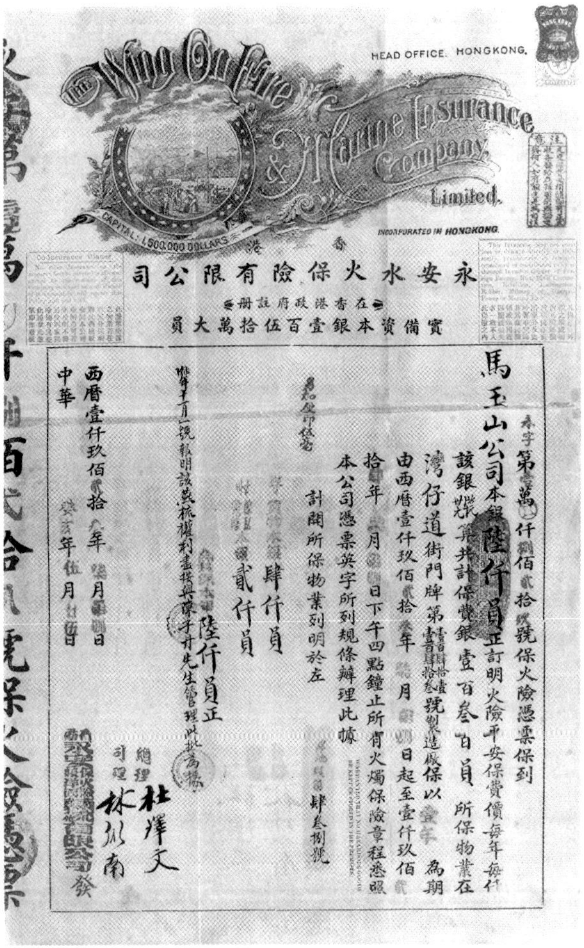

Fig. 2.13
A policy issued by the Wing On Marine Insurance Co. in 1923.

The year before the Japanese Imperial Army invaded Mainland China, Gocklock left for the United States to expand his business there. But once the Japanese moved on to take over Hong Kong, he was marooned overseas. All of Wing On's operations were thus under Gockchin's watch. Wing On Life carried on under the most trying of circumstances in the occupied colony.

On 15 August 1945, the Japanese surrendered and the occupation came to an end. Gocklock and his son, Lam Po, returned to Hong Kong and reorganized the family business. After a half century in business, Wing On was about to turn a new leaf. The civil war in China and the founding of the new regime forced all the mainland stores to close. Wing On thus focused its growth on its home turf and in Southeast Asia.

The Establishment of the Chinese Insurance Association of Hong Kong

To counter the dominance of foreign insurers in the local market, Chinese-owned firms decided to join forces and strengthen their connections with one another. Together, in 1903, they formed the Chinese Insurance Association of Hong Kong. At its founding, twelve companies came on board. Membership was granted only to companies, not individual agents. Today, the association remains as one of the city's oldest trade groups.

The position of chairman was not established until 1919; the first vice-chairman was named in 1942. Every year, member firms took turns to take the association's helm.

During its first few decades, the association's agenda was light, comprised mostly of charity functions and industry-wide social events intended to develop business opportunities. Some of the group's most important tasks were setting the fire premium rates in Guangzhou and submitting comments on the Macanese government's insurance regulations.

As soon as the association resumed business after the Japanese occupation, it set up a sub-committee to handle matters related to fire products. In the postwar years, the group played an important part in providing smaller member firms with a mechanism for reinsurance.

Over the last half century, the group has remained close to its mission: to defend members' rights and interests. It has also played an active role in improving professionalism and the quality of service within the industry.

The Insurance Industry during the Japanese Occupation

After 1937, when the Mainland fell into the grip of defensive warfare against the Japanese, the development of insurance (and of all other industries) was stunted. Meanwhile, insurance continued to flourish in Hong Kong; combined annual sales in between 1938 and 1939 were more than $300 million. That was until 1941, when the Japanese invaded the colony as well. During a takeover that lasted three years and eight months, all businesses withered.

As soon as the Japanese took control of the colony, all foreign insurers saw their assets liquidated, while the Chinese-owned firms were ordered to carry on business as usual. However, the business climate was unusually trying. According to a brief company history

Fig. 2.14
The Japanese occupation dealt a blow to all industries in Hong Kong, including insurance.

compiled by Sincere, citizens in occupied Hong Kong lost faith in the future and were far more concerned about staving off hunger and staying alive than taking out life policies. On top of that, they were forced to trade in their dollars for Japanese military yen.

Fortunately for Sincere, most of its assets were in real estate and were spared from liquidation.

Its peer, Wing On, also toughed out the occupation period. After the war, the military yen became worthless. Yet, Wing On still accepted premium payments in yen. The insurer wrote off its losses and won praise from clients.

Chapter 3
Post–World War II Rejuvenation and Transformation

The history of the insurance market in Hong Kong can be traced back to the 1940s when fire was the main line of business, followed by marine. In those days, insurance business was run on a 'compradore' basis, i.e. a commission agent was responsible for business production as well as premium collection.

> Following the change of government in China, there was an exodus of industrialists from the Mainland to Hong Kong and the ports in China were blockaded. With the help of the expertise of these immigrants, Hong Kong became industrialized and its unrivalled position as entrepôt for China's imports and exports created large volume of shipments. The export business demand and the commercial and industrial premises development increased by several folds. The risks in construction and shipping thus attracted foreign insurers to enter the market. This boom extended across the 50s and 60s. During this period, the Hong Kong insurance market was dominated by foreign companies, particularly U.K. companies operating through their branch office or agents. These agents were and are still managed by the insurance departments of some of the big Hongs, such as Jardines [*sic*], Matheson, the Swire Group and Inchcape Group. Nevertheless, local companies were able to expand and prosper consequently.
>
> — Louis Sze Ki Kwon,
>
> *A Study of the Profits of Local General Insurance Companies*, 1987

The Insurance Industry's Postwar Reconstruction and Development

On 7 December 1941, the Japanese attacked Pearl Harbor and occupied Shanghai's International Concession. World War II thus spilled into the Pacific theatre. By Christmas day, Hong Kong was invaded. The war nearly destroyed a century of painstaking effort among British firms in Hong Kong and China. The colony's insurance sector was not spared the havoc.

In face of imminent invasion, foreign insurers made plans to suspend business and retreat from Hong Kong. In January 1941, Union moved its headquarters from Hong Kong to Sydney, setting up an office at the City Mutual Building, 60 Hunter Street. The relocation decision had been approved by the board of directors only a year before. In hindsight, the board's chairman, J. Dickson Leach, affirmed that this decision helped save the company.

Once the war broke out in the Pacific and Hong Kong fell to the Japanese, Union's staff in Asia gradually retreated to Sydney. Tokio Marine & Fire Insurance Company, once Union's primary source of re-insurance business from Japan, stepped up as agent for the company in Hong Kong. During the war, Union lost almost all of its records, saw its property ravaged, and suffered heavy financial losses.

During the occupation, Canton Insurance's employees likewise relocated to Sydney, and its London office took over the operations in Hong Kong and maintained the company's connections in the region. Other foreign insurers either retreated from the colony or suspended business. The insurance sector ground to a halt.

On 15 August 1945, the Japanese surrendered unconditionally and the war ended. Hong Kong's postwar economy recovered, and businesses flourished. This ushered in a new phase in the development of the insurance industry.

Foreign insurers returned to Hong Kong and the Mainland to resume operations. In 1946, Union Insurance recovered part of its assets locally and in the Far East and saw its business rebound quickly. The company's balance sheet was restored to its prewar shape. 'Fantastic', exclaimed Union's chairman, Frederick Tout.[1] The headquarters returned home to the colony.

By July 1947, just as Union had completed its return, its Asia-Pacific employees hurried back to the headquarters to clean up the mess. In that same year, Union's premium revenues swelled from £3 million the year before to a record £4 million. The company brought in auditing firm Lowe, Bingham & Matthews, which it had used previously, to straighten the books by reclassifying some of the company's reserves as paid-up capital. In 1948, Union again raked in record premium revenues, its assets exceeding £10 million.

Before the war, for most insurers, especially the foreign firms, the focus of their business had been on Mainland China. So after the war these foreign insurers tried to return to the Mainland to rebuild their operations. In 1946, Union's E. A. Brodie was assigned to Shanghai to pick up where the company left off.

Brodie, a manager originally based in Bombay, had been arrested by the Japanese army in December 1941 while on business in Shanghai, and was held there until the end of the war. Once freed, Brodie went to inspect the office and found it expropriated by a staff member of the Greater East Asia Co-Prosperity movement. The office otherwise had remained intact, except that 'we had to start practically from scratch as all our records were gone', said Brodie.[2]

Next, Brodie travelled on the Royal Navy and U.S. Navy vessels to Beijing and Tianjin to examine Union's offices there. The Tianjin office had been occupied by the Japanese and emptied of records; the Beijing office had been converted into a curio shop.

Union resumed operations in its Shanghai and Tianjin offices. But as the Nationalist Party was losing ground in the civil war, the volume of insurance business dwindled. By 1950, the year after the People's Republic was founded, Union shut down both offices and relocated all its mainland business to Hong Kong.

Union took over the China Fire Insurance Co. in 1951 and, in 1953, renamed its Yangtze Insurance Co. the 'North Pacific Insurance Co'. Union's chairman J. D. Alexander said the roaring river namesake no longer carried the same cachet as it had in the past.[3]

Canton Insurance also ceased its mainland operations in 1949. At one time, mainland business accounted for about 60% of the company's revenues. But one Canton employee recalled how the spiralling inflation of 1947 caused the Chinese currency to depreciate rapidly, such that shoppers had to carry large wads of cash. Housewives often lugged canvas bags full of bills on their grocery shopping trips.

Jardine Matheson's employees in Shanghai got paid three times a month, but the Chinese currencies they received were depreciating by the minute. So on every payday they would rush out to spend the money as fast as they could, or their families would come collect the money and go on a shopping spree, before the paycheque shrank even further.

In 1954, Canton Insurance, renamed Lombard Insurance since the year before, officially closed its office in Shanghai, marking the end of the company's century-old operation on the Mainland. With the loss of the bulk of mainland business, 'Canton Insurance' was by then a misnomer.

The Lombard name originated from the street where Jardine Matheson, Canton's parent company, based its London head office. Its headquarters at 3 Lombard Street has stood for more than a century; in 1894 Jardine even gave the name to an insurance subsidiary.

The history of the name goes back still further, to 600 BC. Back then, a Germanic tribe invaded Italy and where they settled in the north became known as the Lombard duchy (or the Lombardy region in Italy today).

In medieval times, the duchy's growth concentrated around Milan and Genoa, two thriving business centres. Soon enough, Lombard emerged as an important centre for innovation and worldwide transactions, as well as a hub for advanced development in banking and accounting. When traders and bankers from Lombard migrated to London to expand their business, the street where they congregated was nicknamed 'Lombard Street'. The name stuck, and lives on to this day.

Fig. 3.1
The Union Building in Central, c. 1950s. The Union Insurance Society's offices were on the first floor.

Later, as the trading empires along the Mediterranean withered and the British economy blossomed, Lombard Street became the global banking and insurance centre. The credit goes to the Germanic tribesmen from Scandinavia, who invaded Lombardy circa 500 AD, because it was their descendants who developed modern banking and bookkeeping know-how.

The 1950s witnessed significant changes in the global political and economic landscape. Growing nationalist sentiments in developing countries took the shape of greater restrictions on foreign vessels and insurers. Some of these nations actively developed their own national fleets to get their share of 'invisible income from shipping'. Others, in an attempt to foster domestic financial enterprises, limited the types of marine products foreign insurers could legally offer.

In 1962, Union's chairman, J. F. MacGregor said, 'The Society, with its worldwide network of branches and agencies, is affected by these restrictive influences.'

Nigel Rigg, manager for Union's marine department, put it this way: 'The 1960s were years of great changes in the commercial world in the East and I believe the Society showed the way, certainly as far as the insurance industry was concerned.'

Driven by unimpeded nationalist sentiments, governments in Burma and Ceylon (as Sri Lanka was then known) shut down Union's operations. By 1964, the Jakarta office was closed and did not reopen until five years later. Union's branches in Asia dwindled down to ten.

Given the obstacles to growth on the Mainland and in Asia as a whole, Hong Kong's foreign insurers began to explore the markets in Australia, North America, and North Africa. In 1950, Union opened branches in Toronto, Montreal, Calgary, and Winnipeg, thus strengthening the company's presence in Canada. By then, the Beaver Fire Insurance Co. of Winnipeg, acquired in 1920, was fully incorporated into Union's operations. Between 1952 and 1953, Union expanded into Africa with branches in Cape Town, Bulawayo, Durban, Mombasa, and Nairobi.

In 1957, the face value of Union's shares was £10, with a net asset value per share at around £28. Because Union became known as 'one of the world's most expensive insurance stocks', the board split the shares into £1 each so as to attract more shareholders.

In 1960, Union accepted a takeover by London's Guardian Assurance. 'It would be true to say that the Guardian's approach to the Society was not unwelcome,' Union's chairman, Percy Dunt, later would say. 'The Society, although very sound financially, was finding its relatively small size an increasing handicap when competing for the insurance business of the fewer and fewer but larger commercial and industrial companies around the world.'[4]

By 1966, the number of Union's branches in Canada expanded to eighteen, spread across eight provinces. The expansion also took place in Oceania: Union had seven branches each in Australia and New Zealand by 1964.

To be sure, Union was not about to give up on Asia. At that time, many Asian countries encouraged, or even required, foreign firms to enter into joint ventures with local enterprises. The goal was to support homegrown business development and investment and expedite the transfer of technology and management know-how to local executives.

Hence, in 1975 in Indonesia, Union established a new joint venture, P. T. Maskapai Asuransi Union–Far East. Even in its founding year, the new enterprise showed tremendous promise, with an extensive network of branches being built up. 'We were the forerunners in forming joint ventures with local participation in the markets in which we operated,' said Rigg, who was by this time Union's chairman. 'Despite some misgivings in London, the Society formed its first joint venture in Indonesia in 1975 and this has proved to be successful over a period of years.'

Rigg continued: 'Perhaps more importantly, the Society began actively looking for nationals of the countries in which we operated to become executives of the Society. This was a conscious corporate strategy of the Society to identify more closely with the territories in which we made our money.'[5]

At the same time, Lombard (formerly Canton) also was aggressively expanding overseas. It first targeted Australia, where it had strong ties with three firms, each a century old and each with a significant local presence: Jardine Matheson, George King & Co., and the South Australia Insurance Co. A founder of George King was employed by Jardine Matheson in Guangzhou in 1827. Two years later, while visiting Sydney, he set up an agency, which afterward acted as an intermediary between Jardine and Australian firms. With this connection, insurance coverage could be provided by Magniac in Calcutta, India.

In 1881 Canton Insurance (later, in 1953, called Lombard) was incorporated in Hong Kong as a limited liability company. George King and its partners held some of its shares. In 1888, George King was appointed as official agent for Hong Kong Fire. This business relationship was maintained until 1893.

In 1964, Lombard acquired the Thacker Co. of Sydney, and set up branches in major parts of the country, such as Perth (1967), Melbourne (1969), Queensland (1972), and South Australia (1973). Some of these branches were established through acquisition of other insurers' local agents.

In the 1950s and 1960s, Lombard's operations expanded swiftly in Japan, Southeast Asia, and Europe. The company's organization had evolved from a network of overseas agents and branches into a conglomeration of shareholding entities, such as in Hong Kong, Malaysia, and Korea. By the mid-1980s, Lombard had Hong Kong as its base and subsidiaries all over the globe, including Japan, Korea, the Chinese Mainland, Singapore, Thailand, Malaysia, the Philippines, Britain, Australia, and New Zealand. An international insurance conglomerate thus came into being.[6]

The Development and Transformation of the Postwar Insurance Sector

After three years and eight months of Japanese occupation, Hong Kong was liberated by the Pacific fleet commanded by Lt. C. H. J. Harcourt of the Royal Navy on 30 August 1945. The fleet docked at Victoria Harbour, and colonial rule resumed.

'While the harbour thundered to triumphant salutes of every warship[,] on land, rubble, dissolution, disorder and hunger were everywhere to be seen,' according to one contemporary account. 'The harbour was jammed with sunken vessels. The population has been reduced by a million and most of those who remained had no money, no home, no food and no fuel.'[7]

The Royal Navy personnel who arrived set up a military government, but when the wartime governor, Sir Mark Young, returned in May 1946 from Japanese imprisonment, he re-established the civilian administration.

During that time, Hong Kong's economy remained crippled, inflation deepened, unemployment was rampant, food and commodities were lacking. Once the colonial government resumed control, it introduced a series of measures to restore political and economic order.

By 1947, the political situation in Hong Kong had stabilized, and private businesses picked up where they left off. The colony's traditional function as an entrepôt was revived. On the eve of the Japanese invasion, in 1939, the total volume of cargo in and out of Hong Kong's port was about 2 million tons. But by 1947, the volume had spiked to 3.3 million.

In that same year, the volume of external trade was valued at $2.77 billion, more than double the prewar (1931) volume of $1.28 billion. In 1951, the volume soared to $9.30 billion, a 236% increase from 1947. The reason behind this exponential growth in trade volume lay on the Mainland. Since foreign firms such as Jardine Matheson and Swire had retreated from the Mainland, the young republic was hungry for economic ties with the outside world. So Hong Kong filled the role of intermediary, with foreign firms there thriving on the Mainland's growing demands.

The brief period between the end of World War II and the start of the United Nations embargo on China was the heyday of the marine sector. Coverage for imports and exports was in demand. Given the small number of established insurers, competition had yet to turn fierce, and margins were good. In those days, intermediaries benefited from both soliciting business and collecting premiums.

Good times do not keep rolling forever. When the Korean War broke out in 1950, the United States prevailed over the UN to impose an embargo on China. This dealt a huge blow to Hong Kong's trans-shipment business, with a domino effect on shipping, finance, insurance, and other sectors. After 1952, marine products led in the long slide in the insurance sector, with sales shrinking by as much as 20% to 30% in 1954. The hardest hit was marine coverage along the South Asia route, especially in Indonesia and Thailand.

Beginning in 1952, Indonesian government required all imports to be insured by domestic firms. This nearly spelled the end for marine business for foreign firms. Political turmoil and trade restrictions in parts of Asia had also adversely affected Hong Kong's foreign trade and, indirectly, its marine insurance business.

Fig. 3.2
Cheung Sha Wan, a thriving manufacturing district c. the 1950s.

In the marine sector, the trade routes that yielded the most business included those to the Chinese Mainland, Thailand, Singapore, Malaysia, and Japan. Although individual policies on these routes were not huge, the business was frequent and stable.

Of these routes, that to the Mainland generated the most business, but competition on that route was also increasingly fierce. From 1955 to 1956, the war insurance premium for mainland customers was slashed four times, from $3 per $100 of coverage to 25 cents on every $100. But all was not lost. The lower premiums on marine and war products brought down the costs of doing business and hence stimulated more trade. This resulted in a greater flow of business from the Mainland.

Even so, the pie of marine business was not big, with more and more insurers trying to get a slice of it. Most exporters would get insurance at the countries to which they were shipping, while importers would get their goods insured before they reached Hong Kong. As competition heated up, insurers pulled out all the stops. For example, some extended the grace period for premium collection from the standard one to three weeks to as long as six months for clients in good standing. Others hired go-fers and agents and paid them hefty commissions for soliciting businesses. This enticed more foreign trading firms, and traditional Chinese savings and loans were entering the fray. Still others would undercut rivals with deeper and deeper discounts and even offered paybacks to clients.

At that time, most insurers shunned, or rejected outright, business from certain ports in Africa and South America. Due to the high risk of theft there, insurers faced greater chances of incurring losses. Some insurers would charge higher premiums, but they could barely cover the payouts. But premiums on certain routes were already at rock bottom. For example, in 1952 British routes charged about 0.25%, which meant 25 cents on every $100; the Japan route commanded 0.15%; for Africa and South America, depending on the circumstances, it could run to $7 or $8 or even $10 per every $100 of coverage.

Fig. 3.3
A car pile-up in North Point, 12 June 1966. Hong Kong had been pelted by unusually heavy rains, resulting in landslides, collapsed roads, traffic jams, and school and factory closures.

In a 1955 report, Union's chairman C. Blaker emphasized the 'chronic competitive nature' in the marine business, saying there was a 'scramble for business' and 'indiscriminate rate-cutting' going on.

From the late 1950s to the mid-1960s, Hong Kong succeeded in transforming its economy from a traditional entrepôt to a light manufacturing centre in the Far East. Toward the end of 1940s on the Mainland, the Communists and the Nationalists broke into a third battle. The unstable political situation caused a throng of industrialists to flee Shanghai and other cities for Hong Kong. These refugees packed with them the essential ingredients for industrial development: capital, know-how, equipment, and business contacts worldwide. All this allowed them a fresh start in manufacturing business. First it was textiles, then clothing.

Also, Hong Kong had all the favourable conditions that enabled industries to flourish: a simple tax structure and low rates; liberal financial policies allowing unfettered capital flows; advanced telecommunications infrastructure; first class port facilities, and abundant cheap labour. In 1959, local exports rose to $2.3 billion, and trans-shipments to a record $2 billion. All this signalled that the economy was well on its way to industrialization. In 1960, total foreign trade was valued at $9.8 billion, far surpassing the 1951 record level.

The rapid export growth naturally lifted the boat of the marine insurance business. But Union's chairman, MacGregor (chairman, 1957–1965), pointed out, 'Competition for marine business is possibly keener now than it has ever been in the postwar years with rates at a dangerously low level.' J. Dickson Leach, MacGregor's successor as chairman, said, 'The immediate outlook for marine insurance is poor.'

In the 1960s, marine insurers were dealt blow after blow. In 1962, Typhoon Wanda ravaged the colony, resulting in 120 deaths, 20 capsized vessels, and enormous property losses. Insurers doled out damage payments in the hundred of thousands of dollars. In 1965, Typhoon Betsy engulfed Hong Kong again and resulted in a record payout for a single policy.

PUI CHUNG COLLEGE

Fig. 3.4
The damage caused by Typhoon Wanda in 1962 cost insurers dearly.

Union already paid out at least 85% of its premium revenues in 1964, and nearly 90% in 1965. Members of the insurance trade associations reached an agreement in 1964 to fix the premium rates.

Mother Nature aside, politics also intervened. The influence of the Cultural Revolution on the Mainland seeped into Hong Kong. First, it started as the Star Ferry riot of April 1966, then it took the form of unrest at a plastic-flower factory in San Po Kong, and, finally, a full-blown political riot engulfed the colony in 1967. In these troubled times, export-import trade was delayed and marine insurance business affected. And when the workers' and sailors' unions struck, cargo handling at the dockyards was paralyzed. Marine insurance demand fell nearly flat.

Figs. 3.5 & 3.6 (top)
Riots in 1956 cost factory owners heavy losses and persuaded many of them to get coverage.

Fig. 3.7 (bottom)
Military policemen in North Point during the period of martial law in 1967. The riots that year hit the colony's economy hard.

Fig. 3.8
A police raid on a union hall in August 1967.

Marine insurers began to impose a surcharge on older vessels to bring in more revenues. Beginning in March 1967, some older craft saw premiums increase fourfold, from 0.75% to 3%.

The riots of 1967 sent Hong Kong's economy down a slippery slope: real estate value plummeted, emigrants left in droves, and middle-class policyholders suspended coverage or sought loans to cash in on the paid-up value. The shortage of U.S. dollars in circulation in the market compounded the difficulties. James Wong, who joined the American International Assurance Co. Ltd. in 1967—he advanced to general manager for the Hong Kong region in 1987—recalled that because the policies stipulated that all payouts be made in U.S. dollars, to satisfy the demand of all the clients AIA had to ship in US$250,000 from the United States in order to overcome the crisis.

Once the crisis was over, AIA hoped to relocate its operations near the continental United States, but somewhere with British law. Bermuda was just the place. AIA became the first local life insurer to incorporate there. In fact, AIA incorporated in the name of a subsidiary, the American International Reinsurance Company. Many other foreign life insurers followed suit. This resulted in what Wong called 'the Bermuda enigma'.

James Wong
Former CEO, Dah Sing Life Assurance Co. Ltd.
Joined the industry in 1967

When I first started, my family members frowned upon my decision to join the sector, but then I ended up staying on for more than forty years. During the decades, only once did I think of quitting the business.

I was giving out a cash payment to a family member of a policyholder. As he was counting the bills, the family member suddenly burst out crying, so much so he wasn't able to count anymore. I was baffled, and asked myself: 'Why should he be so upset? Is insurance so much a bad thing that causes such sadness?'

Gripped by that thought, I wanted to quit. But later, my superior explained that upon receiving the payout, the family of policyholder is invariably reminded of the departed. They've got the cash in hand but no longer their loved ones. So they just can't help it. Once I understood this intricate chain of reactions, I decided to stay on—to this day.

The 1968 blockade of the Suez Canal, a result of the Six-Day War between Israel and Egypt, cast a long shadow on the global shipping trade. When it was over, the oil crisis reared its ugly head in the 1970s and 1980s, and an unprecedented wave of inflation soon followed. The oil crisis paved the way for high-tonnage tankers. Ironically, as recently as the 1950s, Union's chairman, MacGregor, pointed out that 'tankers of a capacity [were] unthought-of as being practicable a few years ago', because their high costs 'produced problems for underwriters'.

In fact, in the two decades that followed, a series of tankers was christened around the globe, not just supertankers of 500,000 tons but also super-sized bulk carriers and globular liquefied petroleum gas carriers. As the tonnage rose, so did the risks. Frequent oil spills and messy cleanups courted stiff opposition from environmentalists. The sector also was laden with anxiety by these giant tankers. However, by the 1970s, insurers realized that these tankers merely changed the scope of coverage for policyholders and brought in higher margins. That was because containerization had helped reduce losses through theft and damage.

But the fire insurance business was thriving, when compared with the ups and downs in marine. When the Korean War broke out in early 1950s, foreign trade shrank and with it the marine business. However, the demand for fire coverage surged as more unsold goods were put into storage.

In hopes of attracting more fire business, firms began to hire agents by the dozens, if not by the hundreds. To compete, firms also handed out handsome commissions to brokers and discounts to clients. Taking all that into account, insurers raked in 65% to 70% of premium revenues. The more established firms with a deeper client pool tended to get the upper hand and reaped higher margins. Newcomers often lost out in such a competitive environment and closed down for lack of liquidity. Some clients would even divide their fire coverage into a few smaller chunks among various insurers to placate competing firms.

Figs. 3.9 & 3.10
The red-covered 'Bible': *Tariff of the Fire Insurance Association of Hong Kong*, at left; at right is its index page.

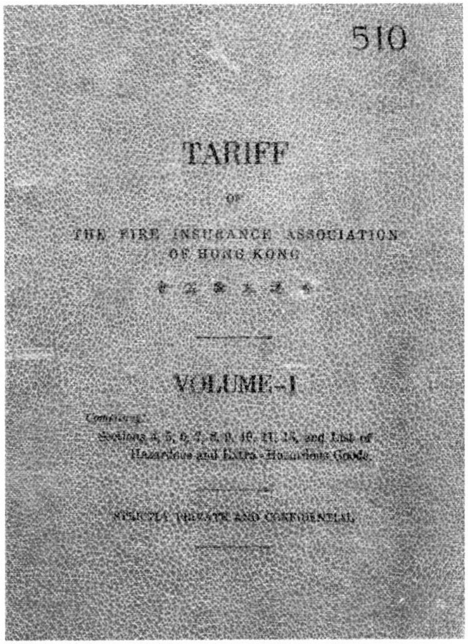

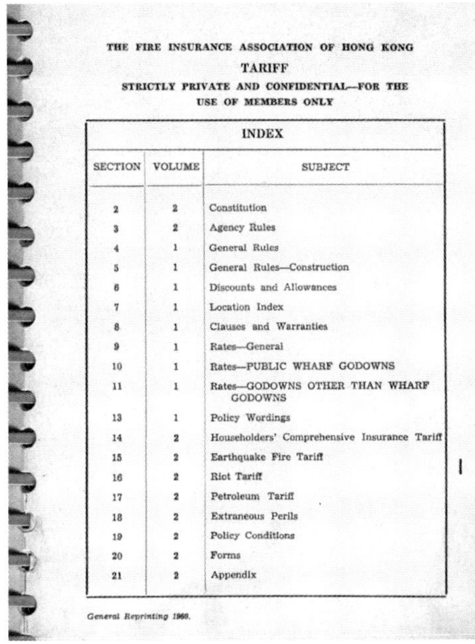
THE FIRE INSURANCE ASSOCIATION OF HONG KONG
TARIFF
STRICTLY PRIVATE AND CONFIDENTIAL—FOR THE USE OF MEMBERS ONLY

INDEX

SECTION	VOLUME	SUBJECT
2	2	Constitution
3	2	Agency Rules
4	1	General Rules
5	1	General Rules—Construction
6	1	Discounts and Allowances
7	1	Location Index
8	1	Clauses and Warranties
9	1	Rates—General
10	1	Rates—PUBLIC WHARF GODOWNS
11	1	Rates—GODOWNS OTHER THAN WHARF GODOWNS
13	1	Policy Wordings
14	2	Householders' Comprehensive Insurance Tariff
15	2	Earthquake Fire Tariff
16	2	Riot Tariff
17	2	Petroleum Tariff
18	2	Extraneous Perils
19	2	Policy Conditions
20	2	Forms
21	2	Appendix

General Reprinting 1960.

According to practitioners, a firm could previously break even on $300 million worth of polices, but by 1961 it would require $400 million of business. To attract more business, insurers offered premium discounts. For instance, firms charged about $3 for every $1,000 of residential fire coverage, plus a surcharge of $1 or $2 if the policyholders lived next to factories with inflammatory materials. Lots of firms would waive this surcharge to win clients. So, on the surface the 1963 fire rates remained stable, but the discounts were not. The discounts ran at 30% to 35% in 1962 but up to 40% to 50% by 1963.

In the early 1960s, tariff (premium) rates for fire coverage ran the gamut from 0.18% to 2% or 3%, depending on the covered environment and its amenities. Rates for shophouses could go from 0.18% to 0.6%. Most policies expired after one year.

Fig. 3.11
Firefighters deploying a 'turntable ladder' at a plastics factory, October 1970. Fires were frequent as Hong Kong industrialized in the 1960s and 1970s.

Not long afterwards, the Fire Insurance Association of Hong Kong began to publish the *Tariff of the Fire Insurance Association of Hong Kong*. Dubbed 'the Bible' by industry practitioners, it listed the rates for every type of fire coverage. All FIA members had to charge the published rates. The FIA revised the rates annually; however, the big British firms got the most say as to the adjustments; others had no choice but to go along with it.

As the number of marine and fire policies grew, many insurers began to establish a re-insurance system to spread risks among peers.

In Hong Kong, the re-insurance system was bifurcated: consensual and mandatory. In consensual re-insurance, for every high-value policy a firm issued, it would be responsible for the entire coverage, but a percentage of the coverage, on a case-by-case basis, would be assigned to a partner firm. With mandatory re-insurance, firms entered into mutually binding long-term contracts, which stipulated a fixed portion of a certain type or line of coverage. Parties to the contract would audit their accounts every month.

But frequent fires in 1961 meant a heavier payout burden on the insurers. For example, the cotton cargo in the Kowloon Godown caught fire quite a few times. After every incident, investigators from the insurance company would look for inadequacies in the storage facilities that may call for higher tariffs, but they had no luck. In 1966, of the more than 2,700 reported fire incidents, 150 were serious blazes and cost $10 million in damages for the insurers. In 1969, the number of reported incidents jumped to 5,105, a 25% increase over 1968, and cost $20 million in payouts.

The reasons the fire business thrived in the 1960s are as follows: (1) The blazes that broke out from 1960 to 1963 had seriously damaged shops and homes alike; insurers used the incidents to solicit more clients and issue more commercial policies. (2) As trans-shipment activities intensified, packed warehouses were often vulnerable to fire; and as factories received more orders for their products, they put away more raw materials and inventory for storage and sought more coverage. (3) There were more new buildings and hence more candidates for fire coverage.

Table 3.1. Hong Kong Insurers in the Early 1960s

Year	Number of Members				
	MIA	**FIA**	**AcIA**	**CIA**	**Total no. of insurers**
1959	107	80	87	20	N/A
1960	117	123	96	21	157
1961	119	129	99	21	160
1962	119	130	100	24	160
1963	119	132	105	25	160
1964	119	151	116	26	160

MIA : Marine Insurance Association of Hong Kong
FIA : Fire Insurance Association of Hong Kong
AcIA : Accident Insurance Association of Hong Kong
CIA : Chinese Insurance Association of Hong Kong

Source: *Hong Kong Economic Yearbook*, 1960–1965

Fig. 3.12
Cars on Garden Road in Central, 1962. The Motor Vehicle Insurance (Third Party Risks) Ordinance went into effect as the number of cars and auto accidents rose in the 1960s.

Apart from fire insurance, accident products were also in demand. The most popular were car- and work-related. For shops, banks, savings and loans, and jewellers, coverage related to theft, robbery, and transportation were most common.

By the 1950s, as the number of cars and auto accidents grew, colonial governor Sir Alexander Grantham issued the Motor Vehicle Insurance (Third Party Risks) Ordinance and mandated insurance for anyone who controlled a vehicle. The goal was to protect outside parties involved in car accidents. Rates for motor vehicle coverage were set by the Accident Insurance Association of Hong Kong, the AcIA, based on a vehicle's age and horsepower. Because car accidents were frequent, insurers paid out more and more. Motor vehicle insurance became a loss leader. In 1954, one insurer saw an incident rate as high as 60% of the client pool; another paid out half of its premium income.

The AcIA, established in 1946, played its role in uniting insurers that offered accident coverage and instituting a well-oiled system for providing such coverage. It conferred membership on insurers dealing in any kind of accident products. By 1987, 141 firms were members.[8]

In 1966, the AcIA announced a rate increase on all vehicles, since auto repairs costs and payout percentages for third parties both had increased. Full coverage on buses, minibuses, and private cars went up 35%, on motorcycles 15%, and on third-party risks 50%.

Meanwhile, in industrializing Hong Kong, the number of factories and workshops was increasing by the day, and so were industrial accidents. Coverage for workers was gaining momentum. In December 1953, the Hong Kong government enacted the Workmen's Compensation Ordinance, which required all employers to take out policies for all those on their payroll. The ordinance also stipulated rates commensurate with the level of job-related risks. For most employees, the rate was 1%, but it could be as high as 10% for well-drillers, demolition workers, scaffold builders, and the like.

Y.K.LAU
STORE
TAXI
XX 7584
2309
AC 8186
4696

However, only large factories and commercial conglomerates purchased the required insurance, while most of the smaller factories and enterprises in dangerous industries neglected to do so. Disputes over compensation arose whenever there was a job-related casualty. In light of this, in June 1957 the Labour Department ordered employers to take out policies and list the expenses on their books as recurring operating costs.

During that era, certain events served to simulate the demand for accident products. In October 1956, riots in Kowloon caused work stoppages in the entire textiles sector. This set off a chain of events that snowballed into serious losses to the industries, measured in the hundred thousands of dollars every day. To make things worse, the factories' accident policy did not cover riots. Factory owners wised up and took out riot insurance, some with coverage as high as $100 million.

The Dominance of British Firms in the 1960s

As much as the development of the postwar insurance sector included diversification, the roster of major players did not. Even in the late 1960s, the sector was dominated by big British firms, with agencies, a few locally registered insurers, and subsidiaries of foreign firms setting the agenda.[9]

(1) General agents

These were mostly the traditional 'hongs' acting as local agents handling policies issued by foreign insurance companies. They included Jardine Matheson, Swire, the Gilman Group, Wheelock Marden, the Inchcape Group, and some big banks such as the Hang Seng Bank, which, since the 1950s, had begun to build up an insurance department.

At the time, Jardine Matheson was by far the most influential agency in Hong Kong. Kenneth Kwok, who joined Jardine's insurance department in 1968, recalled that the department's office on the second floor of Jardine House (today's Wheelock House) on

Pedder Street was composed of various sections: marine, fire, accident, compensation, marketing, and personnel, with about a hundred employees. Jardine Matheson not only handled policies issued by wholly owned subsidiaries Lombard and Hong Kong Fire, but also acted as an agent for nearly a dozen multinational insurers based in England, Continental Europe, the United States, and Japan.

Jardine's insurance clients at the time were mostly the blue chips and included Hongkong Land, Dairy Farm, China Light & Power, Hong Kong Tramways, Hongkong Electric Holdings, and Hongkong & Kowloon Wharf & Godown. And by the late 1970s, the department grew to roughly 120 members, took in more than $100 million in premiums and became the first local insurer to computerize its operations.

Kenneth Kwok
Chairman, Marsh (Hong Kong) Limited
Joined the industry in 1968

Jardine's business: In the postwar insurance sector many a British firm was flourishing. Jardine owned the most market share, thanks to subsidiaries Lombard and Hong Kong Fire, which specialized in marine products and fire and accident products respectively. At its peak, Jardine also was the underwriting agent for no fewer than fifteen firms

Lombard's legacy: When Lombard was sold to Continental Insurance, it was a deal forged on the green by none other than Jardine's insurance department head, Michael Somerville. The name stayed on until Lombard was sold again, this time to HSBC. In 1996, HSBC finally merged Lombard, name and all, into its insurance arm.

But that was the end of the storied Lombard name. When I founded Falcon, we adopted a British ship logo very much like Lombard's. In fact, the Falcon was the first vessel ever to have entered China's waters.

Hong Kong Fire's demise: CNA became the owner of Hong Kong Fire after acquiring its parent, Continental. CNA even hung Hong Kong Fire's original insurance license—the first ever in the city—in front of its Wanchai headquarters. I tried to buy back the license, but CNA asked me to write a carte blanche for it; I couldn't possibly have done that.

In the insurance sector, only Swire could match Jardine Matheson's scale and strength. Swire has been involved in the business since shortly after it was founded in Shanghai in 1867. In addition to handling coverage for its subsidiaries, such as Taikoo Sugar, Taikoo Dockyard, and Swire Shipping, Swire also represented several British insurers, including the Royal Exchange Assurance Co., the British & Foreign Marine Insurance Co., the London & Lancashire Co., Union Insurance, the Palatine & Atlas Assurance Co., and others.

After World War II, Swire quickly resumed business in the colony. At first, Swire's insurance department had its office at 1 Connaught Road; it subsequently moved to the second floor of the Union Building (later rebuilt as Swire House), facing Jardine Matheson's insurance department right across the street.

Like its arch rival, Swire's insurance department was also organized into several sections, such as marine, fire, accident, compensation, and accounting. There also was a life section, handling the policies issued by China Underwriters Ltd.

George Yan, who joined Swire's insurance department in 1971, recalled that of seventy-odd employees, all were university graduates except for the few foreigners.

Gong Yiu, who was then head of the department, was particularly successful in winning the trust of the big boss because he knew Yiu's father from his days as a preacher in Shanghai. When Yiu attended Cambridge University, he lived at his future boss' home. Under Yiu's watch, Swire's agent pool swelled to 500.

George Yan
Executive director, Chong Hing Insurance Co. Ltd.
Joined the industry in 1971

I learned a great deal during my seven years at Swire, especially about corporate culture. As an English firm, Swire is steeped in the class system. Even toilets came in two classes: one for clerks and managers, the other for high-level executives.

Also, because Swire is a foreign firm, with an emphasis on a systemic approach to management, no one could thrive in the insurance department without a solid understanding of how the industry worked. The younger employees were especially aggressive, often getting in earlier and getting off later than their Western bosses. They sought every chance to show off their talent, so they couldn't wait for their managers to go on vacation and fill their shoes.

We also learned to cover ourselves. We'd keep a memo on every agreed-upon decision in case some colleagues reneged on their word. One superior of mine even kept a carbon copy of every memo.

My Union Days: Within my first three years at Union, I found myself in a totally different milieu. Unlike Swire, Union was more like a family with a long history with all its employees. Working there gave you a sense of well-being and security. Union treated the employees so well that most would recruit their family members to join the firm. So it was common to find three generations of the same family under Union's employ.

Union was never very hard on its employees. Offices closed at 5:15 p.m. and lights were turned off on the dot. Some employees even headed out to the wet market by 3 or 4 p.m. to do grocery shopping and get ready for dinner. No one in the office was trying to get qualifications or get promoted. Even so, those who have served Union over generations have amassed sizable fortunes. I remember once a colleague in accounting, after being chided by a superior, slammed his desk saying that he'd rather quit because his salary wasn't enough to feed his two dogs. It turns out that he fed his dogs American beef. Union was full of people like him, who didn't care much for the work or promotion.

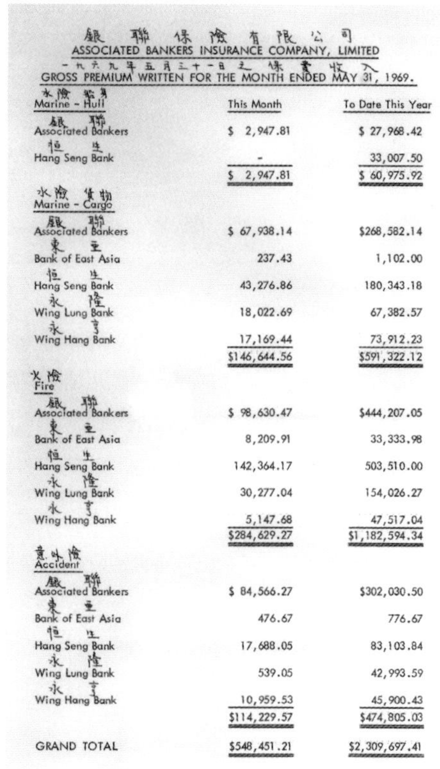

銀聯保險有限公司
ASSOCIATED BANKERS INSURANCE COMPANY, LIMITED
一九六九年五月三十一日之保費收入
GROSS PREMIUM WRITTEN FOR THE MONTH ENDED MAY 31, 1969.

	This Month	To Date This Year
水險船身 Marine - Hull		
銀聯 Associated Bankers	$ 2,947.81	$ 27,968.42
恒生 Hang Seng Bank	-	33,007.50
	$ 2,947.81	$ 60,975.92
水險貨物 Marine - Cargo		
銀聯 Associated Bankers	$ 67,938.14	$268,582.14
東亞 Bank of East Asia	237.43	1,102.00
恒生 Hang Seng Bank	43,276.86	180,343.18
永隆 Wing Lung Bank	18,022.69	67,382.57
永亨 Wing Hang Bank	17,169.44	73,912.23
	$146,644.56	$591,322.12
火險 Fire		
銀聯 Associated Bankers	$ 98,630.47	$444,207.05
東亞 Bank of East Asia	8,209.91	33,333.98
恒生 Hang Seng Bank	142,364.17	503,510.00
永隆 Wing Lung Bank	30,277.04	154,026.27
永亨 Wing Hang Bank	5,147.68	47,517.04
	$284,629.27	$1,182,594.34
意外險 Accident		
銀聯 Associated Bankers	$ 84,566.27	$302,030.50
東亞 Bank of East Asia	476.67	776.67
恒生 Hang Seng Bank	17,688.05	83,103.84
永隆 Wing Lung Bank	539.05	42,993.59
永亨 Wing Hang Bank	10,959.53	45,900.43
	$114,229.57	$474,805.03
GRAND TOTAL	$548,451.21	$2,309,697.41

Fig. 3.13 (left)
The Hang Seng Bank's headquarters, left, late 1950s.

Fig. 3.14 (right)
An Associated Bankers monthly premium statement.

Among the marine insurers, Union was one of the largest and boldest. It tended to go where others feared to tread. During the advent of containerization, most insurers didn't even know what a container was, but Union had researchers in England who pointed out that cargo in containers was less likely subject to damage or theft. Given the lower risks, Union was more willing to cover containers and at lower rates. And when a client suggested that the container be vacuumized in order to maximize tonnage and minimize damage, Union was open to trying this new technique and lowering premiums.

Union enjoyed long heydays. Western employees recalled that when Union moved to Hong Kong it bought land all over the Victoria Peak to build quarters for foreign hires. If Union had held on to all the real estate, it would have been a bigger property owner than Hongkong Land. Many buildings in Central, including Chater House, were once owned by Union.

When I first joined the firm, many Westerners told me that even if Union didn't open for business, its assets could more than support all the employees. It didn't take long for Union's mountain of assets to be levelled: The plots and HSBC stocks were gradually sold off. Its conservative style of operations soon lost big accounts in my time, such as Jardine, Hongkong Electric, and HSBC, to competitors. Ultimately, Union's biggest mistake was to have lost faith in the future of post-colonial Hong Kong. In 1967, the company decided that it had to begin to disinvest in anticipation of the handover and eventually sold to Guardian.

In Hong Kong's banking sector, Hang Seng Savings & Loan (called *'ngan ho'* in Chinese) was the first to launch into the insurance arena. In 1953, Hang Seng officially became a bank and almost immediately set up an insurance department. In 1958, Ko Ying joined the bank as the department's deputy manager but also oversaw marine products. Ko recalled that the department began with a bare crew of five by focusing on only marine and fire lines and acting as Union's underwriter.

Y. Ko
General Manager, KSY Specialty Ltd.
Joined the industry in 1958

How Associated Bankers was born: In 1958, I joined Hang Seng Bank as deputy manager of its insurance department, but I also oversaw marine products. At the time, my department had a skeleton crew of five. We focused our energy and time only on marine and fire lines, acting as Union's underwriter. But by early 1960s, the bank's director, Sin-hang Ho, decided that insurance would grow to be a perennial industry so he set about expanding the operation.

On 15 January 1965, Hang Seng took the lead in establishing Associated Bankers, an entity specializing in insurance, with $5 million in capital. Other banks also participated by buying stakes in the startup, including Bank of East Asia (2% share), Wing Hang Bank (10%) and Wing Lung Bank (20%). Other shareholders were personal friends of Ho and the bank.

Associated was headed by general manager Raymond Kan, a veteran of American International Underwriter, and I became his deputy. Kan's brother Anthony, also an AIU veteran, was of the underwriter of the personal accident department. Its business mostly came from the stakeholding banks, especially Hang Seng's clients.

The Vietnam War also brought business to Associated. Throughout the 1960s and 1970s, Hong Kong served as an entrepôt for supplies, machinery, and equipment bound for Vietnam, while Vietnam's produce and foodstuff exports passed through Hong Kong. Associated charged 1% for comprehensive coverage on trade with all other countries, but as much as 10% (including war coverage) on trade with Vietnam, because the raging warfare posed a much higher risk. So in the late 1960s, Associated reaped huge profits.

Associated's staff grew to ninety employees in the 1980s and was wholly acquired by Hang Seng in March 1993.

> ***Steven Lau***
> ***Independent Non-executive Director, China Region, AXA***
> ***Joined the industry in 1969***
>
> *By the late 1980s, Union ran into financial difficulties and was forced to accept a takeover bid from the Guardian Assurance Group of London. Guardian was a listed company in Britain and ranked among the top five in the global insurance industry. The motivation behind the Union takeover was to use it as a launching pad in the Far Eastern market. That was why Guardian kept Union's name and clientele.*
>
> *But at the end of the day, Guardian's management was never quite able to crack China's market and was reluctant to invest on a large scale. This doomed Union's growth in the 1990s. In 1999, Guardian was acquired by AXA, the large French insurer.*

(2) Locally registered shareholding insurance companies

Among the main ones were Union, Lombard (formerly Canton Insurance), and Hong Kong Fire. However, most of these were controlled by foreign trading or insurance firms. To be sure, there also were a few wholly Chinese-controlled and -funded insurers, such as Wing On Marine & Fire Insurance and the Sincere Insurance & Investment Co. Ltd.

Of all, Union exuded the most influence and strength on the local insurance scene from mid-century through the 1970s. Although traditionally the company's core competency was marine and fire products, it soon dominated the car insurance market in Kowloon, as one of the few insurers with a branch on the peninsula in the 1950s. At the time, nearly all insurers concentrated on Hong Kong Island. When the government mandated insurance for all drivers, long lines formed in front of Union's Kowloon office for motor vehicle policies.

Fig. 3.15
Staff of the South British Insurance Co., 1959, Kam Lung Restaurant, Sheung Wan.

(3) The trend towards consolidation among foreign insurers

Consolidation activities were heated among the foreign insurers that had operations or branches in Hong Kong. What follows are descriptions of the ones involving major players.

Founded in 1872 with New Zealand capital, the Auckland-based South British Insurance Co. Ltd. was so named because Oceania lies on the southern fringe of the British Commonwealth. When South British first expanded to Hong Kong in 1881, George R. Stevens & Co. was its agent. Later, South British set up branches here.

After the Korean War broke out in 1950, supply shipments often passed through Hong Kong, but most insurers were unwilling to undertake the risks. Consequently, South British saw ever more marine business, even at rates as high as 15%, and reaped $3 million to $4 million in premium income a year.

But in 1983, South British was acquired by the New Zealand Insurance Co. Ltd.

H. C. Wong
Non-executive Director, The Ming An (Holdings) Co. Ltd.
Joined the industry in 1950s

War and peace:
The history of the industry has shown that insurers benefit from both war and peace. When the Korean War broke out in June 1950, demand for supplies shot up, but most insurers were unwilling to shoulder the risks of shipping to the Korea peninsula. Those who did charged a war risk premium as much as 15%, much higher than any risk premium we see today.

C. C. Wat
MSIG Insurance (Hong Kong) Ltd.
Joined the industry in 1950

Father-and-son team: Both my father and I worked for South British; our tenures add up to more than half a century. He made it up the rank and file at a major foreign firm because he understood English when others didn't, and he graduated from Queen's College, a prestigious local secondary school.
In that era, people tended to trust foreign firms more than local ones. If you were an exporter who wanted to secure a letter of credit from the bank, most banks would accept only foreign insurers as guarantors.

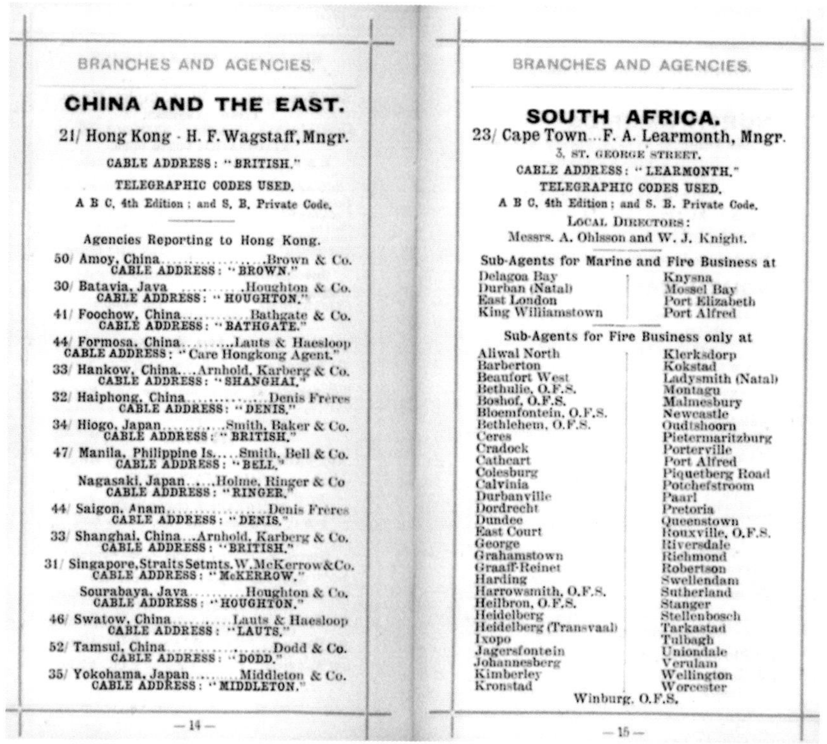

BRANCHES AND AGENCIES.

CHINA AND THE EAST.

21/ Hong Kong - H. F. Wagstaff, Mngr.

CABLE ADDRESS: "BRITISH."

TELEGRAPHIC CODES USED.

A B C, 4th Edition; and S. B. Private Code.

Agencies Reporting to Hong Kong.

50/ Amoy, China.................Brown & Co.
CABLE ADDRESS: "BROWN."

30/ Batavia, Java ....Houghton & Co.
CABLE ADDRESS: "HOUGHTON."

41/ Foochow, China...........Bathgate & Co.
CABLE ADDRESS: "BATHGATE."

44/ Formosa, China.........Lauts & Haesloop
CABLE ADDRESS: "Care Hongkong Agent."

33/ Hankow, China....Arnhold, Karberg & Co.
CABLE ADDRESS: "SHANGHAI."

32/ Haiphong, China.............Denis Frères
CABLE ADDRESS: "DENIS."

34/ Hiogo, Japan...........Smith, Baker & Co.
CABLE ADDRESS: "BRITISH."

47/ Manila, Philippine Is.....Smith, Bell & Co.
CABLE ADDRESS: "BELL."

Nagasaki, Japan.....Holme, Ringer & Co
CABLE ADDRESS: "RINGER."

44/ Saigon, Anam..................Denis Frères
CABLE ADDRESS: "DENIS."

33/ Shanghai, China...Arnhold, Karberg & Co.
CABLE ADDRESS: "BRITISH."

31/ Singapore, Straits Setmts. W. McKerrow & Co.
CABLE ADDRESS: "McKERROW."

Sourabaya, Java..........Houghton & Co.
CABLE ADDRESS: "HOUGHTON."

46/ Swatow, China..........Lauts & Haesloop
CABLE ADDRESS: "LAUTS."

52/ Tamsui, China....................Dodd & Co.
CABLE ADDRESS: "DODD."

35/ Yokohama, Japan.........Middleton & Co.
CABLE ADDRESS: "MIDDLETON."

— 14 —

BRANCHES AND AGENCIES.

SOUTH AFRICA.

23/ Cape Town...F. A. Learmonth, Mngr.

3, ST. GEORGE STREET.

CABLE ADDRESS: "LEARMONTH."

TELEGRAPHIC CODES USED.

A B C, 4th Edition; and S. B. Private Code.

LOCAL DIRECTORS:

Messrs. A. Ohlsson and W. J. Knight.

Sub-Agents for Marine and Fire Business at

Delagoa Bay	Knysna
Durban (Natal)	Mossel Bay
East London	Port Elizabeth
King Williamstown	Port Alfred

Sub-Agents for Fire Business only at

Aliwal North	Klerksdorp
Barberton	Kokstad
Beaufort West	Ladysmith (Natal)
Bethulie, O.F.S.	Montagu
Boshof, O.F.S.	Malmesbury
Bloemfontein, O.F.S.	Newcastle
Bethlehem, O.F.S.	Oudtshoorn
Ceres	Pietermaritzburg
Cradock	Porterville
Cathcart	Port Alfred
Colesburg	Piquetberg Road
Calvinia	Potchefstroom
Durbanville	Paarl
Dordrecht	Pretoria
Dundee	Queenstown
East Court	Rouxville, O.F.S.
George	Riversdale
Grahamstown	Richmond
Graaff-Reinet	Robertson
Harding	Swellendam
Harrowsmith, O.F.S.	Sutherland
Heilbron, O.F.S.	Stanger
Heidelberg	Stellenbosch
Heidelberg (Transvaal)	Tarkastad
Ixopo	Tulbagh
Jagersfontein	Uniondale
Johannesberg	Verulam
Kimberley	Wellington
Kronstad	Worcester

Winburg, O.F.S.

— 15 —

Fig. 3.16
A South British Insurance Co. brochure, 1892.

Vincent Cheung
Agency Development Manager, MSIG Insurance (Hong Kong) Ltd.
Joined the industry in 1970

The merger mania of the 1990s: It was as though every firm was looking to merge with somebody, either to shore up its own position or to pre-empt a hostile takeover. Although at the time the foreign firms were already rather well endowed, most firms thought they could become stronger through M&As and cut down the number of competitors. For instance, General Accident merged with the Commercial Union Assurance Co. Ltd. in 1998. After a short while, the new company merged again with Norwich Union to become CGNU, later called AVIVA.

The New Zealand Insurance Co. Ltd. (NZI)

In the industry, the firm has a storied history: It had covered the *Titanic* and underwrote the damages sustained in the Great Kanto earthquake in Japan in 1923. As early as before World War II, NZI had already expanded its operations to Hong Kong. As light industries—plastics, textiles, and clothing—thrived in the postwar economy, NZI chose to target small and medium-sized enterprises. This strategy paid off, and NZI became a household name in the plastics industry.

Another insurer, the American Foreign Insurance Association, also targeted the same market, while offering the traditional marine, fire, and car products. Its office in Hong Kong also served as the regional headquarters for Asia.

However, by the mid-1980s more and more factories were relocating to the Mainland, and textiles were no longer king in Hong Kong. NZI switched gears and aggressively expanded into real estate and banking, but the stock market crash in 1987 did it in. In 1993, financial difficulties compelled NZI to accept a takeover bid from the General Accident Co.

General Accident, in turn, merged with the Commercial Union Assurance Co. Ltd. in 1998. Established in 1899, Commercial Union also was a firm with a long history and a prominent presence in Hong Kong and Kowloon, with a force of 150 agents. Commercial Union then merged with Norwich Union to become CGNU, later called AVIVA. The merged, restructured firm boasted a team of 250 agents and an annual premium income upward of $1 billion.

In 2005, AVIVA sold its Asia operations to the Mitsui Sumitomo Insurance Co. Ltd. of Japan. The Japanese buyer formed MSIG Insurance (Hong Kong) Ltd. as a springboard to expand its reach in the rest of region.

Fig. 3.17
Staff of Commercial Union Assurance in 1911.

Allan Lam
General Manager, the Sun Chong Fung Insurance Agency
Joined the industry in 1964

Ring of fire: It was a sun-filled day in December 1984, with Christmas just around the corner. A young subordinate reported to me that a barge loaded with firecrackers had burst into flames. I didn't pay much heed because, based on my experience, a barge usually carries cargo worth not much more than half a million.

Ten minutes or so later, another colleague hurried over and said a series of barges had caught fire, all at the same time. Only then did I realize the situation could've taken a serious turn. 'It looks like a ring of fire—on barges,' he quipped.

The fact is, firecrackers are high-risk goods long banned from land storage by a law passed in the aftermath of the 1967 riots. So at the time they were being stored on barges or freighters moored at the waterfront of Sham Shui Po and the Western District. Most insurers were unwilling to cover such cargo, but we did so only as a favour to a long-time client.

At the time of the fire, cargoes of a few barges were unloaded into a container. When the boat full of firecrackers began to explode, the blaze licked the nearby barges and spread unfettered, because these couldn't be steered away on their own power. At the end, as much as $5 million worth of goods were torched.

American International Underwriters Ltd.

Of all the American firms in Hong Kong, AIU was among the oldest and most significant. It had expanded here even before World War II, with its headquarters in Shanghai. After the war, the Hong Kong office became the regional headquarters, overseeing operations in Singapore, Taiwan, Malaysia, and elsewhere in the region.

AIU's product lines included marine, fire, auto, accident, and property. It was the first insurer to adopt a computerized system and trained employees in state-of-the-art sales and marketing strategies. Among foreign firms, AIU was also known to employ local Chinese even in the upper echelon.

W. S. Ching
Experienced practitioner
Joined the industry in 1958

Factory fires everywhere: In the 1970s, Hong Kong saw ever-more textiles factories. Inside, highly flammable cotton bits often littered the floor. It took only a spark to set a place on fire. It was the same with plastics manufacturers, with powdery plastic waste blanketing what could easily—with the help of a stray firecracker from an open window—turn into an inferno.

All these factories became likely clients for various insurers. After securing a promise of damages, it was customary for the factory-owner beneficiary to take out a 'thank you' advertisement in the major dailies. The insurers later caught on and would ask the factory owners to pay for an acknowledgement ad when it came time to cut the cheque. This way, insurers also got some free publicity.

The Sector's Development in the Late 1960s

According to Hong Kong government statistics, there were a total of 207 insurance companies in March 1969. But this figure included many agents and may represent an overstated count.

Another estimate by the *Hong Kong Economic Weekly* showed that, setting aside agencies, there were 167 insurance companies at the end of 1969. An overwhelming majority, 146, offered marine and fire products; the remainder dealt in life products.

Fig. 3.18
A Hong Kong shop floor in the 1960s. The city's booming manufacturing sector boded well for the fire and marine insurance markets.

Of them, British firms accounted for more than a third: sixty-eight. At nineteen, American insurers formed the second largest group of foreign insurers. There were only sixteen locally funded firms. The balance was Asian (including Chinese Mainland), Australian, and Continental European insurers.

O. F. Leung
Chairman, Everbest Insurance Holdings Ltd.
Joined the industry in 1969

Party time: The annual banquet hosted by the Insurance Institute of Hong Kong was a see-and-be-seen occasion for the industry's Who's Who. It also was a time to show off your company's strength. The black-tie event was modeled on that of The Chartered Insurance Institute in the U.K., a traditional English banquet.

The head table was invariably populated with government department heads and CEOs from prominent foreign firms. Each insurer had its own table: The longer the table, the better its show of force. The banquet always began with a toast to the Queen and lasted until midnight over glass after glass. By the 1980s, as the insurers were increasingly dominated by local Chinese firms, standard British colonial fare was no more.

Chapter 4
The Rise of Hong Kong as an Insurance Centre and the Industry's Diversification

> Unlike many other advanced countries, where non-bank financial intermediaries form a significant segment of the financial sector and collectively tend to grow at a faster rate than commercial banks, in Hong Kong the commercial banks still dominate the financial scene, even with the recent emergence of the DTCs [deposit-taking companies]. . . .
>
> The insurance companies are the most important of the non-bank intermediaries. Hong Kong is already a considerable insurance centre: 31 March 1977 there were two hundred and eighty-five insurance companies, of which a hundred and sixty-four were foreign companies, transacting all types of insurance business. This is a natural concomitant of Hong Kong being a major trading, manufacturing, and financial centre.
>
> – Y. C. Jao[1]

Between the late 1960s and the mid-1980s, Hong Kong's economy expanded at a breakneck pace. With the emergence of homegrown stock markets, a whole slew of global financial institutions rushed in, transforming the city into an international financial centre in Asia.

As Yu-ching Jao, a retired honorary professor at Hong Kong University's School of Economics and Finance, has pointed out, Hong Kong's rise as an international financial centre was only one of its two postwar achievements. The other was its successful transition from an entrepôt to a prosperous industrial town. Many locals and even some foreigners would declare Hong Kong as the world's third-largest financial hub, after New York and London. Although this might be an overstatement, according to Jao, suffice it to say it is now generally recognized that Hong Kong is one of the world's major financial centres.

This macroeconomic background has created an excellent business environment for the insurance industry. In the 1970s few Hong Kong laws governed the industry. An insurance firm could open up shop after only making a deposit at the colony's Registrar of Companies.

The lack of foreign currency controls in Hong Kong made it easy to move capital around. The low profit tax rate also allowed firms to build up operating funds relatively quickly. Therefore, it was no surprise that all kinds of insurers flooded the sector, including many from overseas. Even some trading firms, real estate companies, banks, and finance companies joined the fray.

According to data compiled in the yearly *Hong Kong Economic Review*, six new insurers began doing business in 1970, but in 1977 forty-three new companies opened. Of the forty-three, only nine set up head offices locally. This was the year that saw the largest number of new entrants, an increase prompted in part by the government's repeated insinuations that more industry regulations on minimum paid-up capital and solvency margin would be forthcoming.

By the end of the decade, a total of 335 insurers registered for business in Hong Kong, with 203 of them members of one or another trade association. To a large extent, said Jao, 'Hong Kong [has become] already a considerable insurance centre.'[2]

The Diversification of Hong Kong's Insurance Market

As a rash of foreign insurers entered Hong Kong's market in the 1970s, the following structural changes were evident:

(1) Joint ventures between traditional local insurers and foreign newcomers

According to a historical study, 'A major feature of insurance in the Colony is "tied business", especially in the Fire and Marine markets, arising out of their historical

Renewal Receipt

ROYAL INSURANCE COMPANY LIMITED

ROYAL INSURANCE COMPANY LIMITED

Branch Office 903-904, Chartered Bank Building,
Des Voeux Road Central,
P. O. Box 2877,
Hong Kong. Tel. 237128

№ 6590

HONG KONG =0.50 INSURANCE POLICY

In consideration of the payment by the Insured of the premium mentioned hereunder, the Policy referred to is hereby renewed for the period stated

Third Party	Policy No. T.P.1201	Covering the period from / to	23rd December 1971 / 22nd December 1972
Name	The Saddle Club,	Premium	HK$450.00
Address	Lo Wu, New Territories.		
Particulars	Third Party Insurance.		
		Stamp duty	0.50
Sum Insured	£50,000.- (Limit of Liability)	Total	HK$450.50

This receipt confirms acceptance of instructions to continue the Policy and a new Policy will not be issued unless requested. A separate cash receipt will be issued for the payment received.

ROYAL INSURANCE COMPANY LTD.

BRANCH MANAGER

Date 13th January 1972.
j/a.

Fig. 4.1
A third-party insurance policy issued by the Royal Insurance Co. Ltd. in 1971.

development. Every large merchant house is tied up with a favoured insurance company for which it holds the official agency, the connection in some cases going back more than a century'.[3] These large merchant houses, traditionally known as 'hongs', tended to act as agents for the foreign insurers.

However, in the 1970s, some agents began to realize that it would be better for their business if they set up their own insurance firms. So they began to hunt for partners.

In 1971, Swire made plans to establish its own insurance firm. This move was a pro-active response to its clients' desire to deal directly with domestic insurers, instead of a foreign agent that might decamp to its London base at any time. And when Swire learned of similar plans by the Royal Insurance Group, the two joined forces, in 1973, and set up the Royal Insurance Co. Ltd., with the latter taking a 51% stake. By the early 1990s, Royal was the fifth largest insurer in Hong Kong.[4]

Meanwhile, Jardine Matheson, through its insurance department, forged a joint venture with Britain's Sun Alliance Group called Lombard Alliance. In 1976, a longtime agent for the Eagle Star Group, the Mollers Co., formed the Asian Eagle Insurance Co. with the group. In 1977, HSBC re-allocated its insurance business to Wardley Assurance, its joint entity with the Malayan Insurance Co. Inc. Wardley was then re-christened as the Carlingford Insurance Co. Ltd.[5]

Four years before this reorganization, Michael Somerville joined Jardine's insurance department. He recalls the many unprecedented trends shaping the insurance sector in that era.

Michael Somerville
Former Chairman and Executive Director, Lombard Insurance Ltd.
Joined the industry in 1973

The insurance market of the 1970s: In 1973, when I first came to live and work in Hong Kong, the insurance industry was very different than that of today. It was still typical of many of the Asian and indeed colonial markets in that much of its business and practices were dominated by the big general agency houses—the 'hongs', such as Jardine, Swire, and Gilman—representing predominately British international insurers. I recall that we in Jardine represented about a dozen of such companies, of which names such as Alliance, Sun, Commercial Union, Royal, Chubb, and Generali come to mind. Our association with some of these went back a century or more. Behind my desk there hung a framed letter from Jardine to Alliance Assurance dated, as I recall, in the 1860s responding to a request for information on market conditions in Hong Kong on these lines: 'We have made enquiries and have the honour to report that we know of no dangerous substances in Hong Kong other than gunpowder.'

Most of our core business was 'tied', coming from subsidiaries, close associates, customers, and friends of our respective agency houses. I remember that when we bought a controlling interest in Zung Fu, which held then, as it does today, a monopoly on the Mercedes franchise in Hong Kong, being told by my chairman to arrange transfer of all their insurances to us and equally strongly being told by their no-nonsense chief executive to get lost. In the end, a mutually acceptable deal was struck.

Historically, the core insurance business of Hong Kong had been marine and fire and much of the business related to our manufacturing and textile industries. The bulk of this was placed through commission agents, there being no real brokers as we know them today. In Jardine we had a big commission agency department, which principally comprised the professional footballers employed to represent Jardine in the football league, in which we fielded a leading team. Insurance was their second occupation.

Several things combined to change this basic mix of business. Car ownership was growing rapidly, employees' compensation insurance had become compulsory, and major new infrastructure projects were taking place such as the Cross Harbour and Aberdeen tunnels, the High Island [Reservoir] dam construction, and the MTR rail project, resulting in the introduction in the early 1970s of the first contractors' all-risks covers. This business, in particular, together with our growing aviation and shipping industries, brought the big overseas insurance brokers to town with their specialist skills, their access to new markets, and their lack of interest in, even disdain for, old ties and relationships.

Many of our local insurance companies and agencies, lacking the skills and capacity to handle these new challenges, found increasing support and guidance from the international re-insurers, led by Swiss Re and Munich Re. These re-insurers absorbed the lion's share of risk and largely dictated the underwriting strategies of local companies, whose basic risk retentions were often very small, with their revenue principally generated from commissions and property investment. In essence, these big re-insurers acted as midwives and nannies to many such companies.

It was international insurance brokers, above all, who forced the pace of change. When I took over as head of Jardine Insurance I combined the roles of broker, insurer, and general agent, but that was soon to change.

JM. INS DIV
JMIB (HK) LTD.

Fig. 4.2
A painting from colleagues of Michael Somerville when Jardine Insurance Brokers split off as a separate business in 1970s.

In my office, as I write this, is a painting given to me by colleagues when Jardine Insurance Brokers—now JLT—split off as a separate business. It depicts me in a cocked admiral's hat at the stern of a galleon cutting the painter to a rowing boat manned by pirates flying the Jolly Roger—our new broking team setting off to cause havoc to old underwriting traditions!

Whilst the general agencies are now history, they did leave one legacy that has been central in managing the massive changes the industry has undergone and its recent emergence as a major pillar of our financial sector. (Scanning the Hong Kong Yearbooks *from 1973 to 1983 I find no reference to insurance as even being part of our economy!) That legacy is trained professionals.*

The Swiss Republication, Insurance Markets of the World, *published to mark their centenary in 1964, has this to say of Hong Kong: 'There are, as yet, no special training or educational facilities for insurance in Hong Kong. A pamphlet on insurance as a carrier in Hong Kong is in course of preparation.'*

By 1973, Jardine, Swire, and other major players in the insurance market had begun recruiting graduate insurance management trainees from the universities and polytechnics. It is a source of great satisfaction and some personal pride for me that we recruited, trained, and offered international exposure during my time at Jardine and Lombard Insurance to upward of seventy graduates who have pursued their careers to become key players in the industry both in Hong Kong and in China. Many remain my friends to this day. It is they who have faced the challenges of creating new disciplines to replace the outdated rules of the past and have built an industry that is playing an increasingly important role in our social and economic structure.

All that I have written so far is about the general insurance industry. It is in fact the life-insurance industry that has shown the most dramatic growth since my early days in insurance in Hong Kong. The Swiss Re 1964 book I have already quoted said this of life assurance in Hong Kong: 'Life assurance has been slight both because of the protection extended in the Chinese family and in adequate registration of births and deaths.'

One of my main assignments on my arrival in Hong Kong was participation in a project aimed at establishing an all-Asia life insurance company offering investment-linked products to be marketed in Hong Kong through a pension consultancy company and personal financial consultancy company. The two consultancy companies were duly established and became well-known players in their respective fields, but the proposed life insurance company fell victim to the 1970s oil crisis. It was to be another decade before we were able to launch Jardine Life Insurance, later renamed CMG and now part of Sun Life.

But that, as they say, is another story.

As more firms were setting up their own insurance companies, business for agents gradually dried up. And to make matters worse, agents were also squeezed on the margins. As recently as 1972, agents could expect a margin—commission minus rebates to brokers—of 15% to 20%. But by 1977, the kickback rate jumped by 15% or 20% and thereby slashed the margin to 5% at best, and sometimes to close to nothing. So as the agents saw it, the best way out was to set up their own insurance firms and capture all the profits from issuing policies and investing the premium income.[6]

(2) The influx of international brokerages in the mid-1970s

As defined in a directive of what was then the European Economic Community, the meaning of insurance brokers is 'persons who, acting with complete freedom as to their choice of undertaking, bring together, with a view to the insurance or reinsurance of risks, persons seeking insurance or reinsurance to the conclusion of contracts of insurance or reinsurance and, where appropriate, assist in the administration and performance of such contracts, in particular in the event of a claim'.[7]

In other words, a broker is independent of any particular insurer and can freely negotiate with any insurer that offers beneficial terms. A broker acts in accordance with a policyholder's instructions. By law, the broker is agent for the policyholder.

According to veteran broker Sidney Ku, before the 1970s, domestic brokerages were neither visible nor active. Altogether, they accounted for less than 10% of market share, earned mostly as middlemen for small to medium-sized clients.

So when the 1970s ushered in a slew of large-scale infrastructure projects, such as the Mass Transit Railway system, local brokers simply didn't have the wherewithal to offer coverage. That opened up the playing field for large international brokerages. In 1974, two of the world's three largest brokerages, The Marsh & McLennan Cos. Inc. and Johnson & Higgins Ltd., got into the act.

During the early 1980s, Marsh and Sun Hung Kai Properties Ltd. formed a joint venture to set up a local brokerage,[8] but they soon went their separate ways due to a disagreement. Marsh sold its stake to Sun Hung Kai. In 1982, Johnson scored its first local client, the Kowloon-Canton Railways. Meanwhile, London-based Willis Faber and America's Aon also cracked Hong Kong's market.

According to historical data collected by the Munich Reinsurance Co. (Hong Kong), the number of international brokerages mushroomed from six in 1972 to twenty-six in 1977.[9] Most of them were brought in by the big British trading firms to work primarily with British insurers. But other international brokerages also got to monopolize the big businesses of their home countries after they entered the Hong Kong market. For instance, Marsh was made the broker for household American brands such as Coca Cola and Colgate.

Later, even big local businesses, such as Hong Kong and China Gas, China Light & Power, Hongkong Electric, the Royal Hong Kong Jockey Club, and Cathay Pacific Airways, flocked to these international brokerages. As a result, eight to ten such brokerages came to dominate the intermediary market of big domestic corporations and institutions.

The impact of such dominance would continue to shape the sector for a long time to come.

Sidney Ku
General Manager, AMTD Risk Management Ltd.
Joined the industry in 1980

Jardine, the rates renegade: At the time nearly all insurers—except Jardine—would abide by the premium rates set up by the trade group. What Jardine would do was to use the brokers to concurrently negotiate with various insurers on the same contract. Only the insurer offering the best terms would be recommended to the client. Because Jardine dealt with mostly foreign insurers, which tended to blow off the rate guidelines anyway, so sometimes they would even offer rates as low as 20% of the listed rates. Many agents found this disconcerting because they could afford to cut rates by 10% to 20%.

Jardine's tactics helped win it ever-more market share. Other foreign brokerages, meanwhile, also fought to have a piece of the action. All these guys tended to focus on catering to companies from their home countries, not bothering with local businesses.

Needless to say, the local insurers and brokers were not pleased to see that the unfair competition has disrupted what was before a more level playing field. Some began to undercut one another with under-the-table dealings. The tariff rates posted by the trade association gradually became more a relic of the past. The market turned upside down.

(3) Cut-throat competition among the swelling ranks of small and medium-sized local insurers

According to Hong Kong government figures, the number of insurers grew from 270 in 1974 to 335 in 1979, more than anywhere else in Asia.

As the count grew, so did the competition. Some firms would ignore the trade groups' guidelines. They wanted only cut rates and did not make payouts according to protocol. All this may have adversely affected the industry's once healthy growth.

Other firms would compete by offering novel products, such as jewellery coverage, comprehensive retail-store insurance, or life insurance that paid out by installment. As the conventional rates set by the trade associations held less and less sway, insurers saw their premium income plunge. Some, especially fire insurers, began to target small and medium-sized clients, where competition (especially from brokers) was less fierce and margins healthier.

As more and more insurers cropped up, bankruptcy risks for those poorly funded concerns rose. More government supervision became necessary. In 1978, draft legislation on minimum capital requirements for insurers was introduced, followed by many more wide-ranging regulations.[10]

William Woo
Managing Director, the NIU Insurance Agency Ltd.
Joined the industry in 1958

American Asiatic Underwriters: In its early years, AAU got its start acting as agent for American insurers and offering fire and marine products, but soon enough it tapped into the mainland Chinese market and moved its headquarters to Shanghai. But when the civil war broke out, AAU had no choice but relocate its operations to Hong Kong. However, its loyal Chinese clientele—mostly the Shanghai textile moguls—stuck by AAU through thick and thin as they, too, fled the warfare and moved their factories down south to the Crown colony.

Industry Development in the 1970s: Marine and Fire

The 1970s saw a transition in the sector. For most insurers, growth in marine lines slackened and fire products became the mainstay. Motor vehicle, employees' compensation, and other products showed significant growth.

Although in 1970 and 1971 Hong Kong's exports and imports both rose by double-digit percentages, new trade regulations by Western countries resulted in shrinking demand for marine coverage in Hong Kong. Some of these regulations required coverage be offered by the importing nations.

Meanwhile, those years were marked by significant payouts. In the first half of 1971, fires were frequent on freighters transporting cotton. Later that year, Typhoon Lucy wreaked havoc.

In early 1972, the 83,000-ton *Seawise University* burst into flames while undergoing repairs at a Hong Kong shipyard. The payout, in the tens of millions of Hong Kong dollars, was one of the largest in the history of the insurance industry worldwide. But the ship, originally the luxury cruiser *Queen Elizabeth*, was covered by London-based insurers, with only one or two Hong Kong firms covering a small portion. The material impact on the local marine sector was negligible.

The more serious threats stemmed from cargo theft, especially on the Africa and South and Central American routes. To curb losses, insurers raised premiums and limited coverage to 'free from particular average' and 'with particular average'.

The oil crisis of 1973 set off a domino effect that quickly dampened export-import trade in Hong Kong. Marine premium income shrank by as much as 30%, prompted by decreases in both the volume and value of cargo. To compete for the dwindling business, insurers cut rates. Even comprehensive coverage was cheaper than ever.

Fig. 4.3
Typhoon Lucy in 1971 turned the streets under a Cheung Sha Wan flyover into a flood zone. The storm brought heavy economic losses.

After 1975, however, the crisis subsided and the downward trend reversed. But the industry witnessed a rise of dubious claims, which smacked of 'moral hazard'. In 1978 alone, owners of twelve ships submitted claims to insurers that their cargo had been lost at sea. None of these ships filed any accident or casualty report. No wreck or cabin logbook of the ships in question was ever located. The locations of these 'lost' cargoes were in the deepest of oceans, which rendered any attempt at recovery impossible.

ORIENT OVERSEAS LINE

Fig. 4.4
The *Seawise University*, formerly the luxury liner *Queen Elizabeth*, caught fire while docked for repairs at a Hong Kong shipyard in 1972. The payout, in the tens of millions of Hong Kong dollars, was one of the largest in the history of the insurance industry.

Ironically, fire business benefited from some of the adverse economic trends, at least briefly. Inflationary pressure in the early 1970s, a consequence of the oil crisis, helped push up the value of goods and hence rates for fire coverage. In 1972, the Fire Insurance Association of Hong Kong (FIA) raised the minimum premium per policy from HK$20 to HK$30 and later imposed a 30% surcharge on all industrial coverage. The surcharge would remain in effect until April 1978.

Even so, the higher premiums barely covered the mounting number of claims. To cut costs, factory owners often packed the premises with excess inventories and raw materials, many of them inflammable. Inside most industrial buildings, tinderbox-like factories sat cheek by jowl. Poor safety management also added to fire risks.

In 1972, there were 7,677 cases of fire, of which ninety-two were four-alarm blazes. A few of these, factory fires all, each caused more than HK$10 million in damage. As a whole, property losses were estimated at HK$85 million.

But by the mid-1970s, the drag of the sluggish economy finally caught up with the fire sector. The size of policies shrank and premiums fell, except for large-scale factory buildings.

K. P. Cheng
Vice-Chairman and CEO, the China Taiping Insurance (HK) Co. Ltd.
(formerly The Ming An Insurance)
Joined the industry in 1964

When it came to setting rates for fire coverage, the FIA had it down to a science ever since its early days. A case in point: Of all the risk factors set down by the FIA, one was called 'adjacency risk'. By that it meant how likely a factory would be affected by a blaze next door. Insurers determined this risk by examining, among other things, the thickness of firewalls of the factory seeking coverage and the factory's proximity to others. Based on these minutiae, an insurer would set the premium rate accordingly.

In the late 1970s, the world economy showed signs of recovery. A rebound in exports and imports injected renewed momentum into the insurance sector. In the 1970s, the industry's total revenues rose between 20% and 25% every year. And as more residential buildings became available and mortgage lenders mandated insurance for borrowers, business opportunities thus expanded.

Fig. 4.5
Paterson Street in Causeway Bay after an explosion and fire, 1972. Rampant blazes in the 1970s made selling fire products a brisk business — and a mainstay for most insurers.

Growth in Other Product Lines

In 1970, the Hong Kong government issued the Workmen's Compensation (Amendment) Ordinance, prompting many more employers to take out policies and thus advancing workplace safety. However, accidents remained rampant, given the tight workspace and a general lack of safety awareness. Rates of claims were far higher than those for fire and marine policies.

In 1977, the government once again amended the ordinance with requirements for, among other things, severance payments, reimbursement on medical treatment for on-the-job injuries, and a much higher minimum compensation for workers not engaged in manual labour. All this fostered greater growth in this line of insurance.

As Hong Kong's population passed the four million mark in 1972, the number of vehicles neared 190,000, making the territory the world's second most car-saturated place, after Monaco, on a per capita basis. Auto accidents were similarly prevalent. In that same year, 438 people died in nearly 12,800 accidents, the highest toll in a quarter of a century.

The number of private cars plummeted over the next few years, due to higher petrol prices and registration fees, along with doubled parking rental charges. Even so, the number of accidents reached another record in 1977—13,900, a 12.4% jump from previous year. By June 1978, the government mandated third-party risk coverage for all car owners.

In addition to auto accidents, another major threat to life and property in Hong Kong in the early 1970s was robbery. The city was then one of the world's more dangerous, and the crime figures bore out this notoriety. The total number of robberies rose from 7,260 in 1972 to 8,700 in 1973, an astounding 20% rise.

In 1974, costly armed robbery cases included those of the Hong Kong Spinners Industrial Building in Cheung Sha Wan and the Standard Chartered Bank in San Po Kong; each involved losses of up to $1 million. That same year, a jewellery shop at the Hong Kong Hilton Hotel (now the site of Cheung Kong Centre) was robbed four times. In August 1975, $7 million in cash was snatched from Hang Seng Bank's security detail in transit, an audacious act that rattled the city. In light of all this, most insurers handled robbery coverage with extreme care. Some would fold it into fire coverage, or jerk up both the premium and the deductible—or even refuse to write a policy at all.

Also, since 1973 Hong Kong had embarked upon many major infrastructure projects, such as road flyovers, desalination plants, and landmark skyscrapers such as Connaught Centre (now Jardine House). With these came new products such as comprehensive construction coverage and mechanical-engineering all-risks. But only the few most experienced and well-endowed firms could offer this kind of coverage because it entailed a significant amount of liquidity and complex actuarial calculations. At that time, firms such as Munich Re and Swiss Re emerged as the winners.

The Development of Life Insurance from the Postwar Era into the 1970s

Although life insurance had been introduced in Hong Kong as early as the nineteenth century, it developed slowly. Large extended families, conservative cultural attitudes, and a traditional mindset in matters related to life and death made life products a tough sell.

In the 1950s, the city's rapid population surge and economic development greatly expanded the room for growth for life insurance, but the conservative mindset just noted died hard. Most Chinese regarded insurance agents as carriers of inauspicious tidings, or lepers. Indeed, due to a lack of systematic supervision and training, especially among local insurers, many agents ended up selling policies to their friends and family without being able to give them any sound advice. Some of these policyholders ended up with unsuitable contracts and financial losses. This, too, dampened growth in the life sector.

Into the 1970s, the swelling ranks of middle-class families began to improve living standards and increase savings for the future. Meanwhile, the influence of Western ideas was growing while the hold of the traditional extended family was diminishing. More Chinese warmed to life coverage. The period saw the true takeoff of this product line.

At that time, twenty-odd companies were involved in this sector, with Manulife, AIA, and Sun Life the major players. The first two accounted for nearly 80% of the market. But local insurers such as Sincere and Wing On were also doing brisk life business.

Manulife

The first insurer to have offered life products in Hong Kong was the Canadian firm Manulife. Manulife ceased its operations in southern China during the Japanese occupation but resumed business in Central as soon as the war ended. In the postwar years, interest in life coverage was intense and the client pool large. Inquiries came not just from residents in Hong Kong and Macau but also from former policyholders in Shanghai and other mainland cities.[11]

The mainstay of life business at the time was the more Westernized segment of the middle class. This was because ordinary poor folks could hardly afford the premium, while the well-heeled would hardly need that kind of protection.

Just as insurers were trying to recruit more agents, the mores of the time rendered these insurance professionals shysters, or worse. Policyholders were jeered as fools who fell for scams. When he was fresh out of college, Joe Sun applied for an agent's position with Manulife—unwittingly, because in the ad he responded to the company did not call itself an insurance firm. Had he known, Sun, who is now a senior executive consultant with Manulife, said he most likely would not have applied.

Joe Sun
Senior Executive Consultant, Manulife (International) Ltd.
Joined the industry in 1954

English speakers: Armed with an economics degree from a Shanghai university, I ventured to Hong Kong, looking for a better first job. It wasn't easy. Times were bad, as was my Cantonese. But at the time the only people in Hong Kong who could afford insurance were mostly English-speaking higher earners. So my English skills came in handy in helping to win over clients.

My first client: He was a caretaker with the Taikoo Dockyard. He was forty-ish, married, from up north, Shandong Province in China. He had a wife at home and four daughters. He could really use some coverage but he couldn't spare a dime for the start-up premium. So I helped him with the payment at the outset. I came to know his family and afterward got referrals.

I made $400 in commission on this contract; I was beside myself with joy.

In 1959, Manulife's office in southern China was reorganized as its Hong Kong branch. It moved into the Union Building (now Swire House) the next year. During the 1960s, the ranks of agents swelled to nearly forty, from barely a dozen a decade earlier. Through it all, Manulife upheld its standards in training the agents, some of whom sat for exams offered by the Life Office Management Association in the U.S.

Manulife's growth in Hong Kong continued unimpeded into the 1970s. The premium income of the local office, at C$20 million, ranked fourth among all branches. In 1971, it climbed to No. 2. By the mid-1970s, Manulife borrowed a page from AIA's playbook and introduced a system to organize agents and have them answer to respective managers. The system proved essential as the ranks of agents mushroomed to seven hundred by the late 1970s and topped a thousand by the late 1980s. By then, recruiting talent was no longer difficult because Hong Kong society had long shed its prejudice against insurance agents.

Manulife's growth in Hong Kong weathered the economic upheavals of the 1970s. Its products targeted mostly the upper middle class, and contract renewal rates were consistently 90% or above.

The American International Assurance Co. Ltd.

Going head-to-head with Manulife at the time was American International Assurance. Each accounted for 40% of the life sector.

AIA traced its roots to a small general agency founded by Cornelius Vander Starr, an American entrepreneur, in December 1919. Called American Asiatic Underwriters, it was incorporated in Bermuda but headquartered in Shanghai. In its early years, AAU acted

Figs. 4.6 & 4.7
At left, American Asiatic Underwriters in Shanghai. Right, Cornelius Vander Starr, its founder, in 1919.

as agent for American insurers and offered fire and marine products. Two years after its founding and bullish about the life market on the Mainland, Starr tapped AAU's reserves to set up the Asia Life Insurance Co. in Shanghai, the first foreign firm ever to market life products to the Chinese.

Although Asia Life lacked the benefits of precedent and experience, its business grew rapidly. Its offices soon spread across the Mainland, Hong Kong, and Southeast Asia. Such an expansion was made possible mostly by the company's drive to recruit and groom local talent for responsible positions. This soon became ingrained in AIA's corporate culture.

In 1931, Starr founded the International Assurance Co., a conglomerate later known as the American International Group, Inc., with Asia Life absorbed as a wholly owned subsidiary. But that was not all. Before the war, Starr went on to set up eight other firms on the Mainland. Once the war was over, Starr went about rebuilding his business in the Far East, and in 1949 he moved AIG's headquarters to Hong Kong.

Alwin Lam
Chairman, Hong Kong and Macau, the AIA Co. (Bermuda) Ltd.
Joined the industry in 1971

The teething pain of life products: The demand for life products took off in the 1970s, and the decade following was the heyday. At that time, anyone with a dose of diligence and discipline could make it in this business, and you didn't have to be smart.

However, the public had no idea how insurance worked. Insurance companies were way more keen to sell policies than train their agents and brokers. They sold products without clearly explaining how they would benefit policyholders. As a result, many policyholders terminated their contracts. It was a lose-lose situation, and, it hardly bears mentioning, cast the sector in a poor light.

But the sector has made tremendous progress since then. Beginning in 1997, the life sector has faced more fierce competition from banks and because of an ever-growing roster of new products. So we see the need to redouble our efforts to train our workforce and improve customer service. To that end, we have pushed our practitioners to qualify for the Multimillion Dollar Roundtable. Only about 1% of insurance professionals worldwide have earned this coveted credential. By 2008, 1,178 of our local practitioners had achieved this recognition.

By the late 1960s, the iconic AIG high rise was erected on Stubbs Road to house its staff and a sales force of four hundred. By the late 1980s, it had mushroomed to at least 1,700 people.

In the 1970s, AIA introduced a string of life and short-term products with saving elements, ranging from ten to twenty years. These proved wildly popular with clients because they could begin receiving interest income by the fifth year. AIA soon expanded its operations to Malaysia, Thailand, and Singapore, emerging as the leading life insurer in Southeast Asia.

Edmund Tse
Honorary Chairman, The American International Assurance Co. Ltd.
Joined the industry in 1961

Coming home to China: Most people in the industry remember AIA's humble beginnings on the Mainland. But business there was halted after the company's postwar move to Hong Kong. Ever since the reform and opening up of 1980s, Maurice Greenberg, AIA's chairman then, started to make inroads back into China. It so happened that in 1983 I was transferred from Taiwan back to Hong Kong. So I started going with him to the Mainland. Our goal was to re-establish AIA's operations there. For that we went to Beijing at least twice, or even three times a year.

Finally, in November 1991, AIA became the first foreign-owned firm to receive a license in [modern] China. We officially opened for business in Shanghai in 1992.

The Sun Life (Hong Kong) Co. Ltd.

The story of Canada's Sun Life in Hong Kong is emblematic of other companies that entered the life business. Like Manulife, Sun Life also established a beachhead in Hong Kong's life sector early on. It matched Manulife in scope and strength of operations in the mid-1960s. But the riots of 1967 rattled Sun Life's management and they retrenched, only to make a return to Hong Kong in the late 1970s. This wavering caused Sun Life to lag behind other life insurers throughout the 1980s. Sun Life caught up, with the 1997 acquisition of CMG Asia, an Australian life insurer, and became one of the top ten life insurance firms in Hong Kong.

The 1970s also saw an incursion of mainland-owned life insurers, such as PICC, China Ping An, and China Taiping. These mainland startups ushered in innovative products that offered short terms, lower premiums, and quicker yields. Given the wild swings in the Western currency market at the time, the mainland firms attracted customers with their yuan-denominated products, which paid out Hong Kong dollars at maturity.

Anthony Lau
Former President, Sun Life Financial (HK) Ltd.
Joined the industry in 1974

One table fits all: When I joined the life sector, it was a fledgling business in Hong Kong, at best. Since local practitioners didn't have a life table to call their own, they all referenced the one in use in England and the States. So policyholders in Hong Kong ended up paying more than they should. Also, the same table was used for both men and women. The rule of thumb was to take three years off a female client's age. It wasn't until much later that we learned that, on average, women outlive men by seven to eight years.

The Founding and the Functions of the Hong Kong Export Credit Insurance Corporation (ECIC)

Export credit guarantees are used by many governments worldwide to help expand foreign trade by absorbing a range of risks not normally covered by commercial insurers. Such risks are mostly related to currency fluctuations and other factors resulting in non-payment by overseas buyers. This kind of statutory protection has proven an effective measure to promote international commerce.

This system—in the form of the Export Credit Guarantee Department (ECGD)—was invented in 1919 by the British government to encourage traders to export to Australia. So, in the 1950s when Hong Kong's export sector took off and exporters sought similar government protection, they naturally looked to Britain.

The first two people to take this route, in 1961, were G. R. Ross of the Hong Kong General Chamber of Commerce and H. C. Fung of the Federation of Hong Kong Industries. But they were told that under British law the department's scope of insurance was confined to merchants within the country. Not about to give up, Fung and Ross surveyed the membership of their respective groups. Although they garnered only a 10% response rate, they concluded that some insurance trust scheme would be crucial to furthering the colony's export sector.

'The motto for the government at the time was non-interventionism,' said Victor Fung, eldest son of H. C. Fung who sat on the ECIC's advisory board from 1977 to 1982. 'However, my father believed that as export trade was of prominent importance to Hong Kong's small and open economy, it must have its own export credit insurance corporation.'[12]

Besides non-interventionism, the government's neutral stance behooved the export sector to mount a Herculean effort to convince officials and policymakers alike of the necessity of such an entity.

Fig. 4.8
Edmund Tse at a September 1992 press conference. The Chinese government awarded the first insurance license to AIA.

It did not take long for the effort to start paying off. In 1962, Sir Robert Black, the governor at the time, appointed a working group to advise the government on whether or not an export credit insurance scheme should be put in place. The group produced a report, saying that given the commercial and political risks and the market competition faced by Hong Kong exporters, such a scheme should be set up with expert assistance from Britain's ECGD.

In 1964, an ECGD expert completed a report, affirming the necessity for Hong Kong to have its own export credit guarantee mechanism.

Finally, on 23 December 1966, the Hong Kong Export Credit Insurance Corp. was established, with an initial capital of HK$10 million and with the maximum liability backed by the government limited, by law, to HK$300 million. The capital base was raised to HK$20 million in 1973 and maximum liability, by 1977, to HK$2 billion. Although it has government backing for all its liabilities, the ECIC is, by law, an autonomous body operating on a self-sustaining, break-even basis.

Ken D. Robertson, then of HSBC's Malaysia branch, was appointed as the first commissioner of the ECIC. In 1969, the corporation was admitted to the International Union of Credit and Investment Insurers, a.k.a. the Berne Union.

During its first decade, the ECIC offered exporters the following policies:

(A) To cover raw materials, semi-processed items, and consumer goods for which terms of payment are a maximum of 180 days' credit: (1) a comprehensive contracts policy under which liability for these losses starts from the date of contract (comprising all methods of payment); (2) a comprehensive shipments policy, under which liability starts from date of shipment (to cover shipments on documents against payment, documents against acceptance, and open account terms); (3) Comprehensive Cover Policy.

(B) To cover capital goods and production equipment, for which the terms of payment can range from one to five years' credit or longer: (1) a specific contracts policy, covering a single transaction from the date of contract; (2) a specific shipments policy, covering a

Fig. 4.9
The Kowloon Godown, shown here in the 1960s, at the beginning of a dramatic rise in export trade.

single transaction from the date of shipment, and (3) special services policies catering to specific needs of exporters.

The ECIC's job is to indemnify exporters against unpredictable buyer and country risks. Overseas importers might fail to pay or delay payments to Hong Kong's exporters due to bankruptcy, warfare, currency restrictions, the cancellation of import licenses, the imposition of import restrictions, or any number of factors unforeseen at the signing of a contract. During its first year, in 1967, the ECIC's ability to shoulder such risks was seriously tested by a string of untoward world events—the Nigerian Civil War, the Suez Canal blockade, the Six-Day War, and so on. Making matters yet worse, some industrial countries reacted by tightening domestic credit or imposing import restrictions. In the corporation's first fifteen months, it settled eleven claims, six of which related to the Suez closure and the balance caused by buyer bankruptcy.

During the first thirteen years of the ECIC's operations, it insured exports totalling $19 billion. The aggregate premium income for these exports was $90 million, and total investment income for the same period amounted to $24 million. Against these revenues, total claims actually paid, together with the provisions for claims set at 31 March 1980, amounted to $59 million, of which $11 million (nearly 19% of all claims) was recovered. The underwriting reserves at 31 March 1980 stood at nearly $17 million.

The significance of the ECIC in promoting foreign trade was evident from the beginning and was best summarized as follows by Sir Crawford Murray MacLehose, then the governor, at the tenth anniversary luncheon:

> The ECIC, like so many really potent financial organizations, tends to operate outside the limelight, but the role it fulfills is absolutely vital. . . . It is a tribute to the flexibility and responsiveness of the Corporation that over the past decade it has coped so well with the political and economic vagaries attending the world trade.[13]

Chapter 5
The Formation and Evolution of Industry Supervision

> A decade earlier, in the mid-1970s, the industry was very different from what it is today. Life insurance, with the exception of operators representing international insurers catering primarily to the expatriate market, was minimal. General insurance was dominated by a few players, principally large general agencies representing big overseas insurers. Agents were mainly tied and, other than in marine hull, brokers were not a major force. Domestic insurers were struggling for a share of the market.
>
> Prudential regulation and control were almost non-existent and capital requirements for insurers were derisory. One could register and operate an insurance company with a capital sum of HK$10,000, if my memory serves me correctly. Fly-by-night operators without any sense of responsibility either to the industry or to the public cropped up continually. That most sensitive of all insurance buying groups, the motorists, were constant victims. At a time when the rights and interests of the consumer were increasingly coming into focus—the age of consumerism—the public perception of insurance was extremely negative. Alleged abuses and unprofessional conduct were constantly high on the hit list of the new Consumer Council, formed in 1974.
>
> — Michael Somerville,
> *The Story of the Hong Kong Federation of Insurers 1988–1998*

All legal matters related to insurance were dealt with using contractual agreements and common law cases. The earliest government regulations on the insurance industry were embodied in laws governing other economic activities, such as the Companies Ordinance and the Workmen's Compensation Ordinance.

Figs. 5.1 & 5.2
A commercial motor vehicle policy issued by the China Insurance Co. Ltd., 1973–74. Left, cover page; right, inside page.

中國保險股份有限公司

CHINA INSURANCE COMPANY LIMITED

HEAD OFFICE PEKING CHINA

商用汽車保險單

COMMERCIAL MOTOR VEHICLE POLICY

(~~COMPREHENSIVE~~)THIRD PARTY

DELETED

SECTION I. Loss or Damage

DELETED

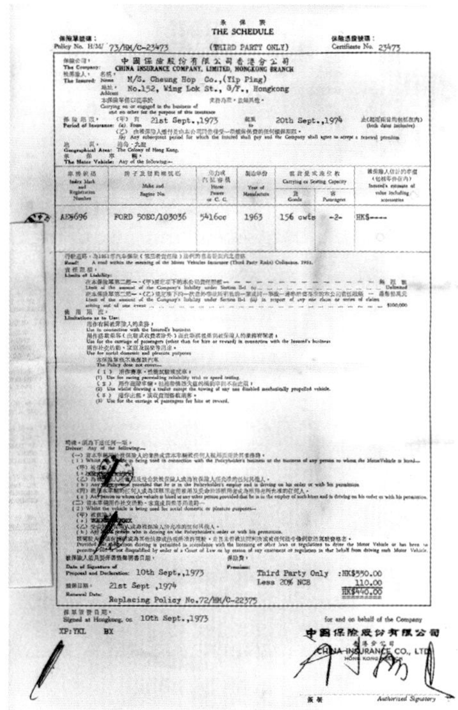

THE SCHEDULE

Policy No. H/M/ 73/HM/C-23473 (THIRD PARTY ONLY) Certificate No. 23473

The Company: CHINA INSURANCE COMPANY, LIMITED, HONGKONG BRANCH

The Insured: M/S. Cheung Hop Co.,(Yip Ping)

No.152, Wing Lok St., G/F., Hongkong

Period of Insurance: From 21st Sept.,1973 To 20th Sept.,1974

Geographical Area: The Colony of Hong Kong

Index Mark and Registration Number	Make and Engine No.	Horse Power or C.C.	Year of Manufacture	Goods	Passengers	Insured's estimate of value including accessories
AE4696	FORD 50EC/103036	5416cc	1963	156 cwts	-2-	HK$----

Date of Signature of Proposal and Declaration: 10th Sept.,1973

Premium: Third Party Only :HK$550.00

Less 20% NCB 110.00

HK$440.00

Renewal Date: 21st Sept ,1974

Replacing Policy No.72/HM/C-22375

Signed at Hongkong, on 10th Sept.,1973

XP:TKL BX

for and on behalf of the Company

中國保險股份有限公司

CHINA INSURANCE CO., LTD.

Authorized Signatory

In the 1950s, the Hong Kong government set about laying down laws for the insurance sector. Hence, both the Third Party (Rights Against Insurers) Ordinance and the Motor Vehicles Insurance (Third Party Risks) Ordinance were enacted. The former guarantees a third party's right to seek compensation in the event that a policyholder or insurance firm files for bankruptcy. The latter is based on the Road Traffic Ordinance, which mandates insurance coverage for all drivers so as to protect the third party's right to compensation in case of accidents caused by drivers.

In 1961, Hong Kong's legislature passed the Marine Insurance Ordinance, based on Britain's Marine Insurance Act of 1906, which was drafted by Sir Mackenzie Dalzell Chalmers, the parliamentary counsel to the Treasury. This act has stood as the model marine insurance act for many other countries.

However, even before the mid-1970s, primarily reflecting its *laissez faire* economic policy, the government's supervision of the sector was rather lax. All it took to start a business was to show some cash, and not much for that matter. A company offering fire or marine products was required to deposit, for each branch, $100,000 in cash or acceptable securities. For life insurers, the capital requirement amounted to three-quarters of the firm's annual premium income, minus claims and losses. A separate fund to meet policy liabilities must be maintained and a quinquennial (decennial for some older, established firms) valuation balance sheet submitted. The required deposit should be no less than $50,000 but not exceeding $200,000.[1] But all insurers may qualify for certain general exemptions if they complied with Britain's requirements for authorization contained in the Insurance Companies Act of 1974.

After the mid-1970s, to groom Hong Kong as an international insurance centre and protect policyholders' interests, the government began to introduce legislation and strengthen supervision on the industry. But before that happened, the number of insurance firms continued to mushroom, from 186 in 1975 to 335 by 1979.

Facing increasingly vociferous criticisms of the insurance sector, the government's regulatory body called upon industry leaders and other veteran practitioners to examine how the industry could be reined in, through both self-regulatory measures and legislative means. After some arduous negotiations, a working group convened by Michael Somerville decided on the three principles that should guide the Hong Kong insurance sector:

- The regulatory mechanism should be tailored for the city's unique business environment and should not be thoughtlessly transplanted from another country.

- Companies need to operate on adequate liquidity, and their boards of directors and executive suites should be filled by fit and proper people.

- The industry should rely on self-regulatory measures as much as possible so that practitioners understand that they have to fulfill responsibilities to society.

After rounds of painstaking deliberation and difficult negotiations with the Legislative Council, the Consumer Council, the banking, accounting and legal sectors, as well as other special interest groups, the first body of regulations was advanced in February 1978. The Insurance Companies (Capital Requirements) Ordinance stipulated that all insurers must have a minimum share capital issued for cash of $5 million. And until the capital was fully paid up, the company could not open for business. This was a rigorous, if onerous, requirement, considering that almost half of the three hundred-plus companies in operation at the time did not put up that much cash. In 1982, the government pushed up this requirement a few notches: The minimum paid-up capital must double, to $10 million.

The regulatory machine did not stop there. In December 1980, the government published in the *Gazette* the Fire and Marine Insurance Companies Deposit (Amendment) Ordinance and the Life Insurance Companies (Amendment) Ordinance, both to be enacted the following month. The amendment ordinances stipulated not only a minimum paid-up capital of $5 million, but also a solvency margin of $2 million (i.e., total assets over total liabilities), and if an insurer offered life in addition to marine or fire products, the margin must be twice as much, $4 million. Insurers offering motor vehicles (third-party risk) coverage must obtain authorization from the Registrar of Companies.

All this culminated in an Insurance Companies bill, a comprehensive body of regulations, first drafted in February 1982. Besides provisions for a higher minimum paid-up, the ordinance also spelled out a more stringent solvency requirement and tighter regulatory oversight. In addition, the government set up an Insurance Advisory Committee (IAC), to be headed by the finance secretary or his representative, to advise on the administration of the legislation. The committee acts as a liaison to represent the industry's interests and provide technical advice and assistance to the authorities.[2]

After more than a year of consultation and revision, the ordinance was put to a motion in the Legislative Council. The ordinance was released in June 1983 and went into effect six months later. The content of the ordinance's sixty-one sections and three amendments can best be summarized as follows:

I. Who is an insurer?
Any firm, group, or individual that applies to operate in the insurance business based upon the ordinance and receives authorization to operate from the regulatory body. According to the ordinance, an insurer can be an insurance firm, a member of Lloyd's, or an organization approved by both the governor and the Legislative Council to offer coverage. Of the three, insurance firms accounted for the most. The ordinance also spelled out that to operate in the insurance sector, a firm or an individual must have an office that deals in insurance and declare to the public this intent.

II. What makes an insurer?
To begin with, all insurers must have a minimum registered capital of $5 million. For those offering comprehensive or statutory coverage, it is $10 million. Insurers must have the financial ability to make payouts. The minimum solvency margin is $2 million for firms whose annual premium income is less than $10 million. For firms grossing $10 million to $50 million in premiums annually, the margin is set at 20% of its income. For all those

bringing in $50 million or more, the margin must be $10 million plus 10% of whatever is in excess of $50 million. Firms offering comprehensive coverage must have a minimum solvency margin of $4 million.

Also, firms must have an adequate arrangement for re-insurance, or a sufficient explanation in its stead. If firms operate in other lines of business outside insurance, they must not jeopardize the policyholders' interests. A firm's name must not be deliberately misleading.

III. Who watches the insurers?

To enforce the new ordinance, the Insurance Authority (IA) was set up[3] to monitor all aspects of an insurance firm, from authorization and operations to financing and liquidation. In order for the IA to get a clear picture of their finances, companies were required annually to file audited financial statements within six months of the end of an accounting period. The insurers must explain the accounting policies used in evaluating each asset and liability and estimating reserves.[4]

Also, companies must submit information on their executives and boards of directors so the IA can make sure they all are 'fit and proper' operators. It has the powers to intervene in a company's operations, when deemed necessary, as it did with thirty-two of them in 1984.

Once the ordinance was enacted, firms complied by shoring up their capital bases. By some estimates, as much as $200 million was injected into the sector by April 1985. A quarter of this new money was raised through share sales; most of the balance was infused by foreign firms.

The new ordinance prohibits life insurers from liquidating at will. Its enactment coincided with the collapse of the Carrian Group. The group rose in the 1970s and 1980s as a property development conglomerate and owned a life insurance company called China

Fig. 5.3
Derek Sullivan, Hong Kong's first insurance commissioner.

Insurance Underwriters Ltd (CIU). When Carrian collapsed like a house of cards in what became the largest bankruptcy case in the history of Hong Kong, the government stepped in to take over CIU for a year before selling it to Sentry Insurance Co. Ltd., which was founded in Wisconsin, US.

In the late 1980s, the government amended the ordinance and shifted the IA from the Registrar General's Department to the Monetary Affairs Branch, where it became an independent entity. This move put the authority on a par with the regulatory body overseeing banks and raised the level of supervision over the sector.

On 8 June 1990, the government officially established the Office of the Commissioner of Insurance (OCI) to administer and amend the ordinance. The OCI was first staffed with two assistant commissioners, for general insurance and long-term insurance respectively. In later years, another one was added to handle policy and development issues.

The OCI supervises insurers through authorization, regulation, intervention, and on-site inspections. The ordinance requires the OCI to extend its supervision not just on insurance firms but also on all intermediaries. Its mission is to ensure that all practitioners conduct business in accordance with ethical and statutory standards. This is done largely through the enforcement of regulations and the promotion of self-regulatory initiatives. Whenever appropriate, the OCI may assist or cooperate with regulatory agencies, local or overseas. A list of all commissioners of insurance follows.

Table 5.1 Commissioners of Insurance, 1990–2009

Name	Years Served
Derek Sullivan	1990–1992
Nigel Shipman	1992–1993
Stephen Ip	1993–1994
Pamela Tan	1994–1995
Ros Lam	1995–1996
Alan Wong	1996–2000
Benjamin Tang	2000–2003
Richard Yuen	2003–2006
Clement Cheung	2006–2009
Annie Choi	2009–present

Source: Office of the Commissioner of Insurance, Hong Kong

The Sector's Self-Regulatory Drive: The Birth of The Hong Kong Federation of Insurers

The enactment of the Insurance Companies Ordinance in 1983 signified that a regulatory regime for the industry was taking shape. Yet, the formation of a self-regulatory mechanism still lagged behind. This mechanism came with the start of the Hong Kong Federation of Insurers, in 1988.

On the occasion of the HKFI's tenth anniversary in 1998, Michael Somerville, the inaugural chairman, vividly recalled the backdrop that gave rise to the organization:

> While regulation of insurance companies and the conduct of their affairs was taking shape, community attention was increasingly being directed at the abuses and

> inconsistencies within the intermediary system, both life and general. Questions were asked as to who was the principal and therefore accountable when things went wrong. The fast growing brokerage community, emphasizing their independence, was adamant that insurers were not the principals. But who were brokers and how could they be relied on to meet their commitments?
>
> Once again the industry found itself unprepared, divided and on the defensive as the Law Reform Commission set up a sub-committee to look into insurance contract law in general and that of intermediaries in particular. From the outset we had to fight a rearguard action against strongly held legal views that legislation should be enacted to follow closely the incredibly complex (and ultimately discredited) control of intermediaries recently enacted in the United Kingdom.
>
> By 1981 it had become generally accepted by insurance industry leaders that something had to be done. The industry was too inward looking, secretive and small thinking. We were constantly on the defensive in the face of growing consumer discontent. We were not chasing opportunities and had an inability to address or articulate our position on broader community issues. We lacked unity and were not pulling our weight in the rapid economic and social development of Hong Kong.[5]

In light of this, attempts were made to unite the sector. In December 1981, plans were made to set up the Insurance Council. Finally, in June 1982, after many rounds of meetings among practitioners, the Insurance Council of Hong Kong was launched. The council's structure and agenda were to be determined by those hailing from various trade groups, including that serving life insurers. The thinking at the time was to build the council up as an umbrella group representing both life and general insurers. (It was renamed the General Insurance Council of Hong Kong in April 1988.)

Fig. 5.4
From left to right, Sir David Akers-Jones, the former chief secretary of Hong Kong; Alex Wong, chairman of the General Insurance Council, and former financial secretary Sir Piers Jacobs at the annual meeting of the Life Insurance Council, 25 March 1991.

K. S. Choy
Former Manager, Committee of The Hong Kong Federation of Insurers
Joined the industry in 1960

Before HKFI was established, there was myriad trade groups in the 1960s. Price Waterhouse [as it was then known] was entrusted with running the secretariat of three of them: the Fire Insurance Association of Hong Kong, the Marine Insurance Association, and the Accident Insurance Association of Hong Kong. These three later formed a committee. Since I was working at Price Waterhouse at the time, I became involved in the committee.

However, given the tremendous growth of the life sector and the prevailing feeling that the council was weighted too heavily in favour of general insurers, the Life Insurance Council of Hong Kong was officially founded in 1984. Each had its own secretariat.

The two councils worked closely on issues related to self-supervision, legislation, intermediaries, and taxation. When the government began to introduce political reforms in the 1980s, talk on the streets hinted that the insurance sector would be made a functional constituency. Yet the existence of twin councils kept any seat out of the sector's reach. This hammered home the urgency for unity.

Meanwhile, the regulatory pressure on the industry kept mounting. In a draft Insurance Companies (Amendment) (No.2) Ordinance published in the Gazette *in June 1986, the government considered raising the capital requirement and invoking a provision that could deny any firm's application to become an underwriter for reasons unspecified. The Law Reform Commission also set up a sub-committee looking into insurance contract law and especially that governing intermediaries.*

In face of all this, the industry realized the need to develop a self-regulatory mechanism—and a united front—was more urgent than ever. So in 1986 the two councils began to take the necessary steps towards a more well-rounded and representative lobby. Within a few months, a working group on self-regulation was formed of local insurers from myriad backgrounds, including British, American, and Chinese Mainland-funded firms. Together, they discussed with the government a mutually agreeable self-regulatory framework that would relieve the need for more stringent legislation.

In May 1987 and January 1988 the Hong Kong Society of Insurance Brokers and the Professional Insurance Brokers Association were formed.

The very group that would finally unite all these industry bodies—the HKFI—was launched on 8 August 1988. Its founding was a milestone in the industry's development. Its mission is as follows:

- Safeguard and expand the common interests of all in the sector;
- Seek common ground on issues affecting member firms' interests;
- Act as the medium for consultation and discussion with the government on legislative and other matters impacting the sector;

Fig. 5.5
The HKFI established its joint offices with the Motor Insurers' Bureau of Hong Kong in the Malaysia Building on Gloucester Road in 1992. Present at the opening ceremony, left to right, were Alex Wong, chairman of the General Insurance Council; Bernard de Petrucci, the Life Council's chairman; Elvon Harris, chairman of the HKFI; Insurance Commissioner Derek Sullivan, and Y. Y. Tang, the HKFI's executive director.

- Promote insurance among Hong Kong residents;
- Devise and implement measures that protect policyholders' interests.

After lengthy negotiation and planning, the Fire Insurance Association of Hong Kong, the Accident Insurance Association of Hong Kong, and the Marine Insurance Association of Hong Kong were brought into the HKFI secretariat's fold on 1 April 1990. Later, representatives of the Medical Insurance Association of Hong Kong, established in 1984, were admitted. All the various technical associations, including the General Insurance Council of Hong Kong and the Life Insurance Council of Hong Kong, eventually merged into the incorporated HKFI on 29 December 1994.

In HKFI's fledgling years, it was actively involved in the government's plan to establish the Office of the Commissioner of Insurance by recommending a division of labour. To wit, the OCI supervised the financial viability of insurance firms but entrusted the federation with matters concerning policyholder interests. Stephen Glanfield, the HKFI chairman from 1988 to 1989, summed up the organization's rationale this way:

> On balance I favour self-regulation where the public interest requires it, but it needs to be remembered the ultimate costs are for the account of the consumer. A proper balance must be maintained.[6]

The HKFI and its Insurance Agents Registration Board (IARB) were given statutory recognition on 30 June 1995. The HKFI would operate as a limited liabilities company. By law, the HKFI is entitled to membership dues and it is authorized to spend the dues only on activities related to goals set out in its articles of incorporation but not on any individual member.

The HKFI is comprised of a governing committee, the IARB, and an appeals tribunal, the last added later to perfect the disciplinary mechanism in place since January 1993. The governing committee is made up of five members each from the General Insurance

Council and the Life Insurance Council, and it is chaired alternately by a candidate from each council. The seventeen-member General Insurance Council includes the AIA, the FIA, the MIA, the Medical Insurance Association and the Reinsurers' Forum, as well as working groups on legal and other matters. The twelve-member Life Insurance Council includes working groups on actuarial work, legal affairs, life risk management, professional standards, and retirement schemes.

The IARB was established on 1 January 1993 and tasked with registering qualified insurance agents, responsible officers, and technical representatives and handling complaints against them. The board provides recourse for insurers and policyholders alike when they feel aggrieved by malpractice. The law requires that all insurance agents register with the IARB.

In its early years, the board was headed by a Legislative Council member, including Elizabeth Wong and Andrew Wong, with the other four members drawn from the Consumer Council, the General Insurance Council, the Life Insurance Council and the Life Underwriters Association of Hong Kong. By 1998, to boost the board's credibility and independence, two members—a barrister and a chartered accountant—were added.

Table 5.2 Chairpersons of the Insurance Agents Registration Board

Name	Years Served
Michael Thornhill	1993–1995
Elizabeth Wong	1995–1997
Andrew Wong	1997–2005
Ambrose Cheung	2005–present

Source: Hong Kong Federation of Insurers

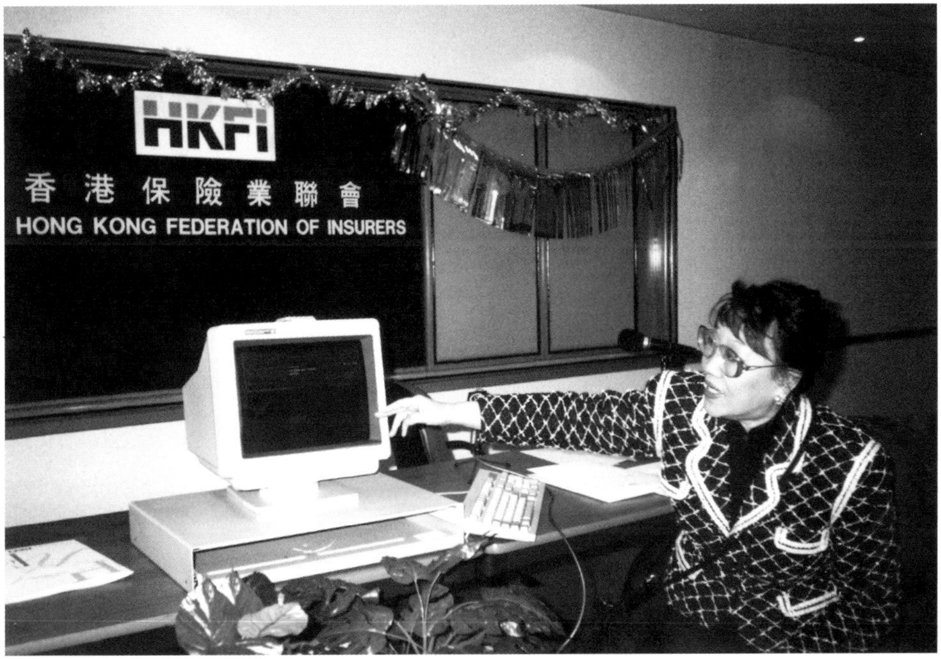

Fig. 5.6
Elizabeth Wong, chairperson of the HKFI's Insurance Agents Registration Board, shows off the new, computerized agents registration system, 19 December 1995.

Development in the 1980s

(1) Internationalization by foreign insurers

Tighter supervision notwithstanding, foreign insurers kept flocking to Hong Kong in the 1980s, mostly because of the market saturation in Western Europe and North America and untapped potential in the city as a rising financial centre in Asia. Plus, the city's *laissez faire* economic policies, the absence of currency control, low tax rates, and developed telecommunications infrastructure all made it attractive to foreign firms.

Between 1983 and 1988, each year saw an average of a dozen or more new foreign insurers applying for authorization from the OCI. By the end of the decade, there were

Fig. 5.7
One of the remaining factories in Kwai Chung, c. 1980s. As manufacturers decamped for the mainland, insurers suffered a loss of business.

altogether 273 authorized insurers in the city, more than half of which—147 to be precise—were foreign firms. They also were the dominant, best-endowed players in the market. Roughly 50 were British firms and 80 American.

To compete better in the global market, in April 1983 Hong Kong's insurers began to adopt the new marine policy language in use in London's insurance market as of the previous year, jettisoning a policy of nearly two centuries old. Not only is the language up-to-date, but the terms are also drastically different.

(2) More products, more training

In an effort to compete in an increasingly cut-throat marketplace, even the more established firms were looking to mine their untapped potential. Introducing new, innovative products and services was one way they sought to maintain market share.

Some insurers tailored new products for specific clienteles, such as mortgage insurance for the growing throng of first-time homebuyers; comprehensive coverage for mom-and-pop business owners, and even personal-safety products for schoolchildren. Other insurers also broke the mold of indemnifying one risk with each policy at a time; they now would offer comprehensive coverage for a range of risks.

Another strategy was to expand avenues for marketing. Firms affiliated with banks would piggyback on their credit-card issuing arm to market insurance products.

The emergence of new products and services called for a better-trained sales force. A new Insurance Training Centre was set up by the government-run Vocational Training Council to expand the council's offerings for the sector's practitioners. Courses were free and of short-term duration, catering to practitioners of different levels of experience and expertise.

(3) Fire margins swell

Throughout the 1980s, fire products remained the bread and butter for most firms. Inflationary pressure helped lift the tariffs and hence swell the margins. At most firms, fire products remained the most lucrative. Helping the bottom line also was the expanding scope of fire coverage, which came to include earthquakes, typhoons, floods, or any post-disaster losses.

Of all fire products, industrial coverage commanded the steepest rates, followed by commercial, with residential the lowest.

The 1980s saw the idea of insurance taking deeper root within the manufacturing and commercial sectors and a higher level of vigilance toward fire prevention. Margins rose as claim rates fell. Still, spectacular damages were inevitable. In 1987, a fire at the Asia TV broadcast building caused damages of $10 to $15 million.

(4) Life products lead the growth

In the early 1980s, only 4% of the population had life insurance, a paltry proportion, comparatively: one in five Singaporeans had some kind of life coverage at this time, and seven in ten Britons. Besides, 90% of the 100,000 businesses in Hong Kong did not offer any kind of retirement plan. Hence, the room for growth proved enormous.

Many firms therefore introduced a whole host of term-life and pension products, targeting mostly the more Westernized postwar generation, people who had the purchasing power and cultural awareness to buy into the insurance market. These customers were much sought after in those days. This kind of intense marketing paid off: The decade added more than half a million new policyholders, and market penetration had risen to 10% by 1989.

The Founding and Operation of the Motor Insurers' Bureau of Hong Kong

In November 1951, as we have previously noted, Governor Alexander Grantham signed into law the Motor Vehicles Insurance (Third Party Risks) Ordinance, requiring all drivers be insured against any claim for third-party bodily injuries or deaths in case of an accident. Yet, there remained cases aplenty in which victims were unable to receive compensation; such cases soared especially with the rapid increase in car ownership in Hong Kong in the late 1970s and early 1980s. This happened when the drivers involved flouted the law and neglected to take out a policy, or when some material breach of policy conditions enabled the insurer to repudiate the drivers' liability. Or, sometimes, the vehicle or driver was plainly untraceable. All this weakened the effectiveness of the ordinance.

Seeing that something needed to be done, the Accident Insurance Association of Hong Kong set about founding an organization similar to the Motor Insurers' Bureau operating in parts of the British Commonwealth. The idea won support from the government, and by late 1979, principles and logistics were agreed upon and the scheme was taking a clearer shape.

Finally, on 27 June 1980, all authorized motor insurers in Hong Kong entered into a 'Principal Agreement' with the government, so committing to establishing the Motor Insurers' Bureau of Hong Kong (MIB) in six months' time.

On 10 December 1980, the MIB was incorporated as a non-profit, limited liability company by government guarantee, thanks to the efforts of 102 motor insurers. But the newly founded entity could not carry out its work until the signing of the First Fund Agreement in February 1981, which gave the MIB the requisite resources and defined its duties. This agreement held the bureau responsible for settling all claims for bodily injury or death as a result of motor vehicle accidents, if the claim was not settled within twenty-eight days from the time of judgment. But the agreement specifically excluded the MIB from liability in judgments that remained unsettled due to the insolvency of an insurer. The First Fund was gradually built up, with a 0.5% to 1% levy on all motor policy premiums.

In addition, the MIB also pledged to abide by the 'Insurer Concerned Principle', which specified that even in cases where there was a breach of the insurance policy conditions, claims for bodily injury or death would still be honoured.

All insurance firms authorized to partake in motor vehicle insurance business in Hong Kong, along with Lloyd's underwriters that were so authorized, had to join the MIB and were bound by this agreement. The government also made MIB membership a condition for any company seeking authorization as a motor insurer. By becoming members,

Fig. 5.8
Brochures published by the Motor Insurers' Bureau of Hong Kong.

insurance firms have essentially entered into an agreement with the bureau to contribute to the fund. New members were required to provide a deed of undertaking to confirm compliance with the domestic agreements upon applying for MIB membership.

A council of seven to eleven members elected from the registered representatives of the membership was to manage the MIB's affairs. They were to meet regularly at the bureau's secretariat at Prince's Building in Central.

Shortly afterwards, in 1983, five motor insurers had their assets liquidated, leaving unsatisfied claims from traffic-accident victims. The government had to deploy public funds to settle these claims.

These incidents prompted the MIB to set up a second fund to meet claims left unsettled by insolvent insurers. The agreement on the insolvency fund was signed with the government on 1 November 1985. It required the MIB to satisfy judgments left outstanding by motor insurers going bankrupt after that date. The fund grew on a 2.5% levy on all motor policy premiums. In 1995, this levy was changed to 2%.

Under English common law, death or bodily injury victims may seek unlimited damages against the wrongdoer, at least theoretically. For many years, motor insurers in Hong Kong had been providing unlimited cover on third-party risks, with help from the re-insurance industry, which offered unlimited protection to the insurers.

By 1994, re-insurers found this kind of unlimited protection unsustainable and informed all insurers that unlimited re-insurance would be discontinued in 1995. This move set off a chain reaction. After rounds of discussion among the government, insurers, and re-insurers, the Motor Vehicles Insurance (Third Party Risks) Ordinance was amended to allow motor-insurance policies covering at least $100 million per event on third-party risks.

However, in the event of an award exceeding the policy's stated limit, the MIB would step up and pay the uninsured portion of a judgment exceeding the policy cover. On 29 June 1995, the bureau provided an undertaking to the government to enhance the First Fund Agreement and take up this new obligation of being the insurer of last resort.

Chapter 6
Changes and Innovations in the Market

In the late 1980s, Hong Kong's economy underwent structural transformation, resulting in the rapid development of the service sector. The insurance industry also entered a period of high growth as insurance gradually became familiar and acceptable by the public. To protect policy holders through effective supervision of the industry, the Government decided to set up a new office with reinforced staff establishment under the then Monetary Affairs Branch to take over from the Insurance Division of the then Registrar General's Department. On 8 June 1990, the Office of the Commissioner of Insurance (OCI) was established.

The past decade witnessed the continuous development of the insurance industry. Premium income increased more than double in ten years, the number of insurance practitioners kept increasing and insurance products became more and more sophisticated and diversified. The OCI has been constantly updating the legislation and introducing appropriate regulatory standards in the light of changes in the market conditions. It has also worked closely with industrial bodies and implemented a series of self-regulatory measures, thus laying a solid foundation for the prudential supervision of the insurance industry.

In the past ten years, Hong Kong experienced many important events, for instance, the return of Hong Kong's sovereignty to China, the Asian financial crisis and the advent of the 21st Century. Of these, the Asian financial crisis has dealt a severe blow to Hong Kong's economy. In a period when the economy experienced a negative growth and a high unemployment rate, the insurance industry was no exception. Nevertheless, our insurance industry as a whole remains financially sound and stable. This is attributable to the effective regulatory system which is the result of the wholehearted collaboration between the industry and the OCI.

— Hong Kong's Commissioner of Insurance, June 2000[1]

Market Transition in the 1990s

(1) Long-term-products earnings beat general

The shift of Hong Kong's economy from manufacturing to services started in the mid-1980s and continued apace into the 1990s. In 1986, the services sector already accounted for nearly 70% of the city's GDP; in 1997, it rose to 85%. By then, the shift was almost complete.

The impact on the insurance sector could not have been more direct. The traditional general products such as marine and employees' compensation, all associated with manufacturing, no longer brought in the most premium. In their stead, long-term products such as life coverage began to rake in increasing revenue. In 1987, general insurance still accounted for two-thirds of the $10 billion in premium income, but its percentage had plunged to 37% by 1997, with life premiums more than picking up the slack. Of the $52 billion in total premium income in 1997, 63%, of $32.5 billion, was generated by life or other long-term policies.

(2) Global firms enter the local life market

Naturally, the booming life market in Hong Kong caught the attention of many global players. Some of them quickly poured in capital and human resources to get a piece of the action. Here we will review four of these new global entrants:

- The Union des Assurance de Paris-Vie, Europe's second-largest insurer, was already offering general coverage in Hong Kong. But in 1991 it made its foray into the life market by focusing on group life and medical insurance products. This yielded remarkable results. In 1994, the company brought out a personal-life and savings product as well as a slew of investment-linked products.

- The National Mutual Life Association of Australia, that country's second largest insurer, raised capital in Hong Kong's stock exchange to expand its operations significantly. As early as in June 1986, Melbourne-based National Mutual acquired the local interest of Sentry Life Insurance (Asia) Ltd. for AUD$58 million and changed its name to National Mutual Asia Ltd. After the takeover, the firm grew from 800 agents to 3,400.

- The Transamerica Occidental Life Insurance Co. traces its roots to Shanghai in 1933. But while the Japanese invasion had scattered Transamerica's policyholders, its staff painstakingly looked for them after the war and carried on with coverage. In 1992, Transamerica built upon this history and its Hong Kong branch to explore markets in the major mainland cities, such as Beijing and Tianjin, as well as Taiwan.

- In January 1995, the Indonesia-based Lippo Group entered the Hong Kong market with the Lippo Reliance Insurance Co. Ltd (formerly the Hong Kong Chinese Insurance Co.), jointly owned by the Hong Kong Chinese Bank and the U.S.-based Protective Life Corp. In addition to conventional life and medical insurance products, Lippo also introduced new investment-linked products to cater to the clientele's needs.

(3) Rampant headhunting in a cut-throat sector

With many foreign insurers flocking to Hong Kong, the already cut-throat sector was getting even more so. As one observer said, historically over half of the insurance market was dominated by a handful of established firms, but as more well-capitalized insurers entered the fray, they were gaining market share by way of financial prowess and marketing strategies. Even so, small and medium-sized operators were digging in and carving out a niche with their diligence and marketing genius. All this made the fight for talent fiercer.

An inevitable outcome was frequent and massive ship-jumping moves, often involving high-level executives decamping to competitors with agents in tow. One such case involved Andrew Yang, who was recruited from National Mutual Asia by Francis Yuen to be executive director of Top Glory Insurance (Bermuda) Ltd. Within two months of Yang's

Fig. 6.1
The staff of National Mutual Asia Ltd. assembled on 8 August 1999 to spell out the insurer's new name since 1999: AXA.

departure, nearly 900 agents from his former firm joined him at the new shop—as well as tens of thousands of policyholders. Before this, Top Glory (formerly New Zealand Life) had but five or six agents and an unimpressive performance record.

This remains the largest-scale personnel move the sector has ever seen. But it did not stop there. Three years later, a twenty-three-year AIA veteran left for Top Glory with more than 140 agents in tow. All this heralded a headhunting trend in the industry.

Andrew Yang
Chairman, the Freeman Corp. Ltd.
Joined the industry in 1957

The dawn of headhunting season: I had bosses who would never hire any agent who ever jumped ship, but I beg to differ. I feel that we live in a free society and, rather, the onus is on the insurance company to hold on to its agents. Not only did I hire agents away from other firms, I also started the practice of transplanting policies from one firm to another.

The way this works is that when agents jump ship to another firm, they take the policies with them. Say, if you've taken out a policy from Company A with an agent who is joining Company B, your policy can be transferred to that company for the same plan and the same cash value. Of course this is bad for Company A and will cause it to lose business, but this cautions companies to treat their people better so as to retain talent and business.

M. K. Cheng
Former Country Manager, ING Asia Pacific
Joined the industry in 1973

The small ups and small downs in life:
The funny thing about the life market is that there never are huge swings, be it up or down. When times are good, it does well. Even when times are bad, business still wouldn't be too bad, so many unemployed would enter the field during economic downturns. If memory serves, premium income for life has been going up every year. The only exception was 2003.

(4) Survival of the fittest

As competition in the life sector grew fierce, it was inevitable that some weaker, smaller firms would feel the squeeze and eventually go out of business. According to data from the Registrar General, the number of authorized insurers gradually shrank from 273 in 1989 to 215 in 1997. That amounts to a 21% drop.

The reasons behind the decrease are many and varied. One reason is that once the foreign firms have gained a foothold in the local market, they sought to consolidate their subsidiaries through mergers. Another is the OCI's tighter supervision.

In April 1992, the OCI notified all authorized life insurers that to keep doing business in Hong Kong they must set up full-service local offices. These had to include executive directors who directly oversaw local operations; a service centre for policyholders to handle matters related to their contracts, and a register of all clients' files. Furthermore, in May 1992, the OCI issued guidelines to life insurers requiring them to document the duties of staff actuaries and actuarial firms under contract. All this served to strengthen the OCI's ability to protect policyholders' interests.

Allan Yu
Director of General Business, The Zurich Insurance Co. Ltd.
Joined the industry in 1969

The Evolution of a European insurer:
Founded in 1875, the Winterthur Swiss Insurance Co. was one of the two major insurers in Switzerland. In the 1970s, Winterthur merged with Britain's Norwich Union and became Norwich Winterthur Insurance, targeting the Asian and African markets. In 1977, Norwich Winterthur Insurance (International) Ltd. was established in Hong Kong, followed by the Winterthur Life Insurance Co. in 1988.

But the Swiss-Brit marriage did not last. By 1991, Norwich Union wanted to quit Asia and sold its stakes in Norwich Winterthur to the Swiss. Winterthur Insurance (Asia) Ltd. thus emerged from this divorce.

Winterthur spared no effort in expanding its Hong Kong operations. In 1992, it acquired Ka Wah AMEV Insurance Ltd. Soon enough, Winterthur cracked the city's list of top ten general insurers.

The Life Market: Innovations in Products, Services, and Sales Strategies

Facing pressures from inflation, government supervision, and competition both internally and externally (from banks branching out into insurance), many life insurers sought to stand out by introducing innovative products and expanding the scope of services.

The following are some of the market innovations that emerged in the 1990s:

(1) Savings and dread disease products

This product line offered the twin benefits of a protection scheme and a flexible savings plan. By making regular premium payments towards this kind of fixed-income investment product, policyholders could build nest eggs and, in the event of an accident, a buffer of protection. They could not only recoup the total amount of premiums but also receive a certain rate of return.

Beginning in the late 1980s, firms such as AIA, Manulife, and National Mutual all marketed a new, terminal illness product. The way it worked was that, unlike traditional life products, which satisfy claims only after the death of policyholders, this product paid out as soon as policyholders were diagnosed with a dread illness. That way the policyholders could use the payout on medical treatment or anything else that might improve the quality of life.

Figs. 6.2 & 6.3
Advertising brochures of Dah Sing Life Assurance and Manulife International.

When it was first introduced, this product line covered only five conditions: cancer, heart attack, coronary artery heart disease, stroke, and kidney failure; later it was expanded to thirty-five to forty more illnesses. In addition, some insurers even paid out dividends more frequently—say, every five years. Others had products with inflation-indexed coverage.

(2) All-in-one coverage

Among the dizzying array of innovative new products, most noteworthy was the all-in-one composite-coverage product. For a single premium, policyholders could enjoy life coverage, protection against illness and accidents, and a premium waiver. And it would be renewable after the customary ten-year term.

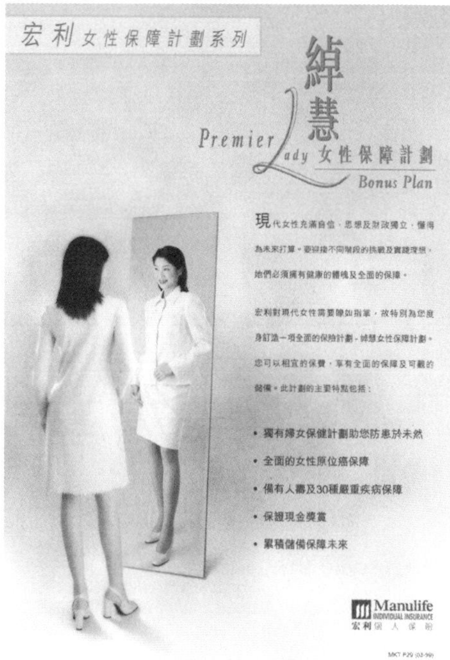

In early 1990s, National Mutual rolled out its 'Smart Lady' plan, with life and illness coverage, as well as investment, all in the same package. This was the first-ever product targeted especially towards women in their fertile years. It covered miscarriage, fetus abnormalities, entropic pregnancy, and other conditions associated with pregnancy, and it did not exclude anyone with pre-existing conditions, including cancer. It proved to be a hit with women and at the time was touted as the best product in Asia. Later, other insurers appealed to a broader clientele by creating coverage for men, women stricken with cancer, and twenty-eight other critical illnesses. The American International Underwriters (Hong Kong) Co. Ltd. even rolled out one single product that covered everything, from emergency care and hospitalization to lost luggage and cash, child care, and personal accidents.

Alvin Li
Chief Executive, The Hang Seng Insurance Co. Ltd.
Joined the industry in 1985

On insurance products: I recalled life insurers introducing dread disease products from South Africa. This product pays out when policyholders are diagnosed with a catastrophic illness pre-defined in the policy. The policyholders can use the payout on medical treatment, to fulfill their lifelong dreams or settle their families financially during the difficult times.

On distribution channels: By the mid-1990s, insurers began to tap into telemarketing. For instance, American International Underwriters (Hong Kong) Co. Ltd. launched its AIU direct initiative to give quotes and sell policies, mostly motor, over the phone. Insurance companies would entice more people to pick up the phone token gifts, such as coupons for baked goods or gasoline.

(3) Combining coverage and investment

In the 1990s, just when the interest rate was lingering on the low end and the government was laying the groundwork for the Mandatory Provident Scheme, a pension fund of sorts, the time for investment-linked insurance products was ripe. Most of these are annuities, but with an added investment component to offset inflation.

The life business remained competitive through the 1990s. Since most insurers found that lowering premiums alone did not do the trick of attracting new clients, they had to stand out of the crowd by doing more. Some did so by expanding their scope of work to insurance counseling, risk management, and investment services. Others even included services totally unrelated to insurance, such as locksmithing, plumbing, housekeeping, and nursing. Most insurers also set up a twenty-four-hour manned hotline to assist policyholders.

And that was not all. Insurers also competed in exploring new sales avenues. One tried-and-true way was telemarketing. This was more than mere cold-calling; it involved a methodical follow-through. Insurance firms would target holders of credit cards issued by banks with which they had a working relationship. After the initial phone call to potential customers, insurers would then mail out brochures and materials detailing insurance product choices. Next, they would follow up with another call to field questions and prompt potential customers to make a decision. This direct mail and telemarketing strategy could yield a positive response rate upward of 25%.

Efforts to seek out more policyholders also prodded more insurers to forge a closer working relationship with banks, especially the few banks that did not have insurance arms. For instance, the Insurance Co. of North America entered into partnerships with Citibank, Standard Chartered, the Bank of China, and others to provide insurance to the banks' customers.

This kind of offering not only benefited the banks but also pleased customers. Since, by law, insurers can partner with a maximum of four banks, they strove to sustain partnerships with superior services.

This sales strategy resulted in simplicity of coverage and ease of payment for policyholders. It also forged symbiotic yet mutually beneficiary relationships between banks and insurers. A further integration of these ties over the 1990s eventually gave rise to a new trend: bancassurance.

Table 6.1 Major Insurers and Partner Banks as of 1990

Banking Group	Insurer
The Hongkong & Shanghai Bank	Carlingford
Bank of China	Ming An, China, and Tai Ping
Hang Seng Bank	Associated Bankers and Union Ins.
Standard Chartered Bank	AIU and Cigna
Bank of East Asia	AIU, Lombard, and Ming An
Dao Heng Bank Group	Dao Heng Insurance
Overseas Trust Bank	OTB Assurance
Shanghai Commercial Bank	Paofoong Insurance
Bank of Credit & Commerce	Commercial Union
Dah Sing Bank	Tugu
Citibank	Eagle Star
Liu Chong Hing Bank	Liu Chong Hing Insurance
Kwong On Bank	Sumitomo Insurance
Ka Wah Bank	Ka Wah Amev Insurance
First Pacific Bank	Far East Insurance

Source: 'A Strategic Study of the General Insurance Industry in Hong Kong', Terry C. S. Yeung, Hong Kong University, unpublished MBA Thesis, 1990, p. 175

Fig. 6.4
A 1993 press conference of the Insurance Claims Complaints Bureau's Complaints Board, convened by Simon Li, the board's first chairman.

Reforms in the Sector's Self-Regulatory System

Since the 1980s, as the supervision regime gradually evolved and matured, professional standards among practitioners improved apace. However, the occasional bad apples, especially in the ranks of agents and brokers, continued to tarnish the hard-earned reputation of the industry.

As early as January 1986, a government-appointed insurance law subcommittee of the Law Reform Commission had already sounded an alarm in a report that explored the feasibility of a system of control for the activities of insurance brokers and agents. The commission recommended that 'anyone seeking to carry on business as a broker be required to register with the OCI. Broking associations would also be entitled to apply for registration, and membership of a registered broking association would automatically satisfy the requirements for insurance registration.

'At the time of the report's publication there was no statutory regulation of the activities of insurance brokers or insurance agents, though insurers themselves were regulated by the Insurance Companies Ordinance. Detailed provisions are also suggested for the registration of broking companies or partnerships, modelled in part on measures contained in the Companies Ordinance.'[2]

Facing a proposal calling for tightening legislation on the sector, industry practitioners submitted a counter-proposal of self-regulatory measures, which was accepted by the government. In fact, the Hong Kong Insurance Brokers Association was very much at the table with the commission beginning in the early 1980s. The Insurance Companies (Amendment) (No. 3) Ordinance, of 1994, reflected the report's recommendations.

Going into the 1990s, and facing mounting pressures from both the public and the legislature, the HKFI was pro-active in building a self-regulatory regime. It sought to phase this in by front- and back-end measures. On the front end, the HKFI asked all insurers to explain clearly to policyholders the terms of the policies they underwrite and make sure customers

INSURANCE CLAIMS COMPLAINTS BOARD
PRESS CONFERENCE

receive fair and reasonable coverage. To that end, in 1990 the HKFI released statements as to the general insurance practice and life practice for all members to abide by.

On the back end, on 20 February of that same year, the HKFI set up the Insurance Claims Complaints Bureau, the first-ever self-regulatory body in the sector, to resolve all claim-related disputes between the policyholder and the underwriter. D. A. C. Nendick, then the financial secretary, touted its founding as a significant step forward in safeguarding consumers' rights and compared it with the insurance ombudsman in the United Kingdom. Nendick said he hoped all registered underwriters would become members of the bureau.

The bureau set up a separate Insurance Claims Complaints Panel (formerly known as the Insurance Claims Complaints Board) to provide independent and impartial adjudication of complaints between insurers and their policyholders or their beneficiaries and rightful claimants. The five-member complaints panel was led by a chairman appointed by the financial secretary. Its four other members included two from within the insurance industry and two from outside.

However, the bureau stipulated that it handled disputes related only to personal insurance contracts but not industrial, commercial, or third-party insurance. And the object of the complaint must be a member. In the beginning, the complaints panel's jurisdiction limit was $250,000. It was repeatedly raised until it reached $800,000 in 2006.

In its early years, only 27 insurers signed on to be members of the bureau. But by 1994, its membership had expanded to a 154 firms, encompassing more than 90% of personal-policy sales value. Later, the bureau made membership mandatory for all registered insurers. Firms could choose to be voting and dues-paying members or opt for a subsidiary and free, non-voting, membership.

Table 6.2 Chairpersons of the Insurance Claims Complaints Bureau

Name	Years Served
Simon Brett	1990–1992
Elvon Harris	1992–1994
Alex Wong	1994–1995
Stephen Moffatt	1995–1998
Terry Smith	1998–1999
Stephen Moffatt	1999–2001
Roddy Anderson	2001–2007
Michael Huddart	2007–present

Source: Insurance Claims Complaints Bureau

Table 6.3 Chairpersons of the Insurance Claims Complaints Panel

Name	Years Served
Simon Li	1990–1994
Henry Wong	1994–2000
Michael Tsui	2000–present

Source: Insurance Claims Complaints Bureau

However, a high-profile case involving an employees' compensation dispute invited the court to challenge the powers of the complaints panel.

In April 1997, a server at a seafood restaurant, Tsoi Hau Ling, took out a policy with Pacific Century Insurance. Ten months later, in February 1998, she slipped and fell at work, injuring her back.

Tsoi suffered back pain but no external signs of injury. But since her Pacific Century policy 'restricted claims for compensation to those where the injury was evidenced by some external manifestation', her claim for $18,000 was rejected.[3]

Aggrieved, Tsoi lodged a complaint with the bureau. The panel ruled in her favour and ordered the insurer to pay the disability benefit she was entitled to under the policy. Pacific Century sought a judicial review of the case.

In its ruling, the court found that the panel's decision went 'behind the terms of the insurance contract'. And in doing so, the panel 'settled upon a policy independent of the terms of contract and/or sound insurance practice, a policy that is founded instead on "sympathy" for claimants who have suffered genuine injury albeit not of the kind allowed for in their insurance policy. . . . Having settled on this policy the Board has then proceeded to incorporate it into its decision-making function'. The court reversed the panel's decision and sided with Pacific Century because it found 'no basis upon which the [panel] could legitimately incorporate such a policy into its function of adjudicating upon current disputes'.

Ultimately, Pacific Century gave Tsoi the full compensation of $18,000, but the ruling alarmed both the OCI and the Consumer Council. The two organizations amended the guidelines to empower the panel to consider other factors besides the policy terms in protecting the interest of policyholders.

The other significant self-regulatory move by the HKFI was to establish a code of conduct for the intermediaries. That became known as the Code of Practice for the Administration of Insurance Agents.

According to the code, 'a person shall not act as an insurance agent for more than four [firms], of whom no more than two shall be long term insurers. If a person acts

Fig. 6.5
Insurance executives at the signing of an agreement on 16 December 1992 to abide by the *Code of Practice for the Administration of Insurance Agents.*

as an insurance agent for any insurer, he shall notify the insurer prior to accepting an appointment to act as an agent for another [firm]. An [insurer] shall obtain the confirmation of the IA [Insurance Authority] in accordance with the code before confirming the appointment of any person as its agent and give the IA details of the registration and cancellation of registration of insurance agents'.

The code was widely regarded as a feat for the sector in championing the rights of policyholders. On 16 December 1992, the HKFI rallied more than 100 members from its subsidiary life-insurance council and general-insurance council to sign an industry agreement to abide by the code. At the time, HKFI Chairman Edmund Tse lauded the agreement as the fruit of three years of hard work in devising self-regulatory measures and a milestone in achieving higher management standards for the industry.

With the agreement signed, the code went into effect in January 1993, and, along with it, so did the new Insurance Agents Registration Board (IARB) under the HKFI. All practising agents had to register at the newly established board by June of the same year but had up to two years to fulfill the minimum requirements. All newcomers, however, had to meet the requirements before entering the industry.

It is estimated that 3,379 general agencies and 22,161 individual agents had registered by the end of 1995.

The IARB also provided for a protocol to handle complaints against agents. Once a complaint had been substantiated by the IARB, the insurer was asked to discipline the agent in question, either by sending a warning letter or by way of license revocation. In 1995, the IARB received 122 complaints involving range of offenses, from providing sub-par service and misleading information to embezzlement and forgery. Of these cases, 48 resulted in the revoking of licenses and 8 in a verbal warning. Considering that there were nearly 30,000 agents, the relatively small number of complaints reflected a high level of self-discipline among the practitioners.

On 18 February 1993, the two trade groups representing brokers—the Hong Kong Insurance Brokers Association, established in 1979, and the Hong Kong Society of Insurance Brokers Ltd., established in 1985—merged, at the government's behest, into The Hong Kong Confederation of Insurance Brokers. With thirty-eight founding members, the confederation's inaugural chairman, Adrian King, welcomed all agencies and individual agents to join, provided that they meet the minimum professional standards. To wit, they had to possess either professional qualifications or years of industry experience, a paid-up capital of $100,000 or more, and professional liability coverage of $2 million or more.

Just when the sector was in full force with its self-regulatory drive, the government also amended regulations to tighten its supervision of intermediaries. The Insurance Companies (Amendment) (No. 3) Ordinance, effective as of June 1995, made a clear distinction between agents and brokers and required each group to get authorization based on applicable regulations.

Under Section 65 of the ICO, 'a person is prohibited from holding himself out as an insurance agent or an insurance broker unless he is properly appointed or authorized. A person is also prohibited from holding himself out as an appointed insurance agent and an authorized insurance broker at the same time. It is an offense under the ICO for an insurer to effect a contract of insurance through, or accept insurance business referred to it by, an insurance intermediary who has not been properly appointed or authorized'.[4]

Other stipulations of the ordinance regarding insurance brokers include these:

- 'A person intending to act as an insurance broker shall either seek authorization from the IA or apply to become a member of a body of insurance brokers approved by the IA.'
- 'An insurance broker who is directly authorized by the IA or is a member of an approved body of insurance brokers is subject to the same statutory requirements.'
- 'For an insurance broker who is a member of an approved body of insurance brokers, he is also subject to the membership regulation of his own professional body which is approved by the IA.'
- 'In order to be authorized as an insurance broker or be admitted as a member of an approved body of insurance brokers, a person, apart from being fit and proper to be

an insurance broker, has to satisfy the minimum requirements specified by the IA with regard to: qualifications and experience; capital and net assets; professional indemnity insurance; keeping of separate client accounts; and keeping of proper books and accounts.'

- 'The detailed requirements on qualifications and experience are set out as follows:

Fig. 6.6
Dennis Pedini, chairman of the HKFI's Life Insurance Council, unveils the *Code of Practice for Life Insurance Replacement* in September 1994.

  - have attained the age of 21; to be a Hong Kong Permanent Resident or a Hong Kong Resident whose employment visa conditions, if any, do not restrict him from being engaged in insurance broking business and to have minimum education standard of Form 5 or equivalent.
  - possess an acceptable insurance qualification and a minimum of 2 years' experience in the insurance industry occupying a management position, or a minimum of 5 years' experience in the insurance industry of which 2 years is at management position.
  - maintain a minimum capital and net assets value of not less than $100,000.
  - maintain a professional indemnity insurance with a minimum limit of indemnity for a minimum of $3 million and a maximum of $75 million.
  - keep client monies in a designated client account separate from his own monies.
  - keep proper books and accounts and other records as will sufficiently explain the transactions and enable a proper audit to be made.'

In response to the amendment ordinance, the HKFI revised its guidelines to familiarize members with the new authorization regulations for agents and brokers, minimum requirements for each group, and principal firms' disciplinary power. That way, the HKFI could also cement its self-regulatory infrastructure with a legislative foundation.

On 28 September 1994, the HKFI's Life Insurance Council announced that, beginning 1 December 1994, the Code of Practice for Life Insurance Replacement would be implemented to control the inappropriate replacement of life insurance policies—i.e., 'twisting'.

The code provided an unambiguous definition of twisting and introduced controls at point of sale by requiring a 'customer protection declaration' to be completed before the client decides to purchase a new life insurance policy. The CPD ensured that the agent had explained to the client all the important consequences, or disadvantages, which were to be put on record in writing for the protection of both the client and the agent.

The code also provided a process, for both the client and the insurer, to assist them in identifying twisting, and to take the necessary action when twisting is identified.

Once it was agreed that twisting had occurred, the selling office had to impose sanction on the agent and reinstate the policy of the client if he so wished. If no agreement was reached, the case was to be referred to the IARB for a ruling.

The LIC's Professional Standards Committee is responsible for monitoring the process and, in extreme cases, can recommend termination of membership.

Dennis Pedini, who chaired both the LIC and its Professional Standards Working Group, said in 1994, 'The code is an extension of the insurance industry's self-regulation. We at the Life Insurance Council will continue our efforts in protecting the rightful interests of the insuring public.'[5]

Then, on 27 June 1996, the LIC announced a cooling-off period of fourteen days following the issuance of a new policy, or twenty-one days following the completion of the application form, whichever was later, to allow a purchaser to re-think his or her decision. If consumers wished to go against the original decision, their policies could be cancelled and they would be entitled to a refund of the premium paid.

For most plans, a 100% refund of premiums would be made to a consumer who exercised the rights within the cooling-off period. No administrative charges would be imposed. For single-premium or unit-linked policies, a market-value adjustment might be applied in the event that the value of the policy has decreased during the cooling-off period.

'The offer of cooling-off rights to consumers is the latest initiative of the Life Insurance Council's self-regulatory programme aiming to give consumers a reasonable period to reflect on their decision before committing to long-term financial plans,' Frank Chan, the LIC chairman, said in 1996. 'I'm very heartened to see that all of our life members have signed the Undertaking to introduce the cooling-off initiative recommended by the Life Insurance Council.'

Ros Lam, the acting commissioner of insurance; and Deborah Glass, senior director of investment products at the Securities & Futures Commission, praised the effort in 1996 as a positive step forward for better consumer protection.[6]

'The standardization of sales illustration for non-unit-linked products coupled with the revised CPD Form demonstrates the LIC's unfailing commitment to develop and support practical consumer protection,' said Alan Wong, the commissioner of insurance, in support of the LIC's initiatives.[7]

'The Consumer Council welcomes the HKFI's adoption of the Code of Conduct for Insurers,' said Anna Wu in 1999, then council chairperson. 'Through the promotion of good insurance practices and market discipline, we believe that the competitiveness of the insurance industry will be geared towards the provision of quality service to the advantage of the insuring public.'

On 7 January 2002, the LIC introduced 'needs analysis initiative' to assist consumers to better understand and evaluate their insurance needs through systematic financial analysis to select insurance products best suited to their needs. By going through the needs analysis exercise, prospective policyholders would be able to prioritize their needs—e.g., future retirement saving vs. current insurance protection, mortgage liability vs. education expenses for children, and so on. Thus, insurance intermediaries would be in a better position to advise prospective policyholders to select the suitable type and level of insurance required.

The LIC's chairperson at the time, Sarah Ho, said in 2002, 'The needs analysis initiative strives to provide a tailor-made service. It is a more customer-oriented approach when compared to the traditional selling approach, which focuses more on the advantages of various insurance products.'

Development and Changes in Hong Kong's Reinsurance Market

The reinsurance business, nearly as old as the insurance industry, got its start in the fourteenth century. Its beginnings can be traced to a 1370 policy issued by an Italian marine insurer to transfer risks to another insurer. A reinsurer is thus, in essence, an insurer's insurer. A reinsurance deal is struck when a reinsurer agrees to compensate an insurer, in part or in whole, the coverage it has extended in underwriting a policy.

The reinsurance business transcends borders. To lower risk, an insurer is free to enter into agreement with reinsurers anywhere in the world. Reinsurance grew briskly from the late 1980s to the late 1990s. Worldwide, net reinsurance premiums jumped from US$29.4 billion in 1988 to nearly US$90 billion by 1997, an average annual increase of 15%.

Also in 1997, reinsurance business coming from direct insurers amounted to US$124 billion, of which 83% was general insurance and the balance life and health.

In the insurance sector of the 1990s, when mergers and acquisitions ruled the day, reinsurance was no exception. Many insurers sought to globalize their operations through takeovers, thus ramping up competition and market dominance. The world's top five reinsurers carved out 43% of the market in 1997, compared with 36% in 1987. Nowadays, some of the most active reinsurance markets are London, Munich, Paris, Zurich, New York, Tokyo, Singapore—and Hong Kong.

Piggybacking on the rapid growth in the insurance sector, reinsurance, too, has found tremendous room for growth in Hong Kong. But its development has not been without challenges.

In the mid-1990s, international disasters and accidents plagued the world, and inflationary pressures bedeviled Hong Kong; claim amounts went up and up. All this made for tough going for the global reinsurers. Some even called it quits; others tried to pull through by raising premiums, being more selective, and shrinking their scope of coverage. It did not help that auto theft and employees' compensation claims both rose at an alarming rate during those years.

So, beginning in 1995, some reinsurers no longer accepted unlimited-liability employees' compensation and motor policies for coverage. By some estimates, the total gross and net premium revenues for reinsurers in 1994 were $2.51 billion and $2.19 billion respectively. In 1998, those figures plunged to $1.75 billion and $1.57 billion respectively.

With contraction came concentration. In 1998, Hong Kong's top ten reinsurers captured a 45% market share. By 2005, the top five—China International, Munich Re, Swiss Re, Toa, and Transatlantic—swallowed 82% of the market. Munich Re and Swiss Re are among the world's largest reinsurance firms.

Against all odds, Hong Kong has emerged as a reinsurance centre. By the end of 1998, it had twenty-eight authorized reinsurers, according to data from the OCI and Standard & Poor's. This put the city in second place in Asia, behind Singapore.

In terms of types of coverage, property loss accounted for 48% of total net premiums, followed by proportional/quota share (19%), motor vehicle (7%), freight, and medical (6% each).

The potential for development in Hong Kong's reinsurance market remains robust. On its side are advanced transportation and telecommunications infrastructure, the relative abundance of talent, and proximity to Chinese Mainland, Taiwan, and Japan—the three large markets. The only downsides are the high cost of operations and the 16.5% profit tax levied on all reinsurance revenues.

Beginning in the mid-1990s, the government stepped up its drive to turn the city into a global reinsurance centre. In his 1996 budget speech, Donald Tsang, then the financial secretary, articulated the government's desire to diversify the city's insurance interests. To that end, a working group was convened to explore the possibility of making Hong Kong the Asia-Pacific region's reinsurance centre and fostering captive insurance business.

Captive insurance refers to an insurer established by its parent company for the sole purpose of underwriting exclusively the insurance business of the parent or all its affiliates. According to the Insurance Companies Ordinance (Cap. 41), a captive insurer can indemnify its parent, subsidiaries, and all affiliates and can also take its business to outside insurers.

Andrew Chow
General Manager and Chief Underwriting Officer,
The Hang Seng General Insurance (HK) Co. Ltd.
Joined the industry in 1982

Captive fight: Although, by the mid-1990s, both Hong Kong and Singapore were vying to be the captive-insurance centre of Asia, ultimately the Labuan federal territory of Malaysia came out a winner. That was mostly because in October 1990 Labuan was officially established as an international offshore financial centre—or, more bluntly and plainly put, a tax haven.

The concept of captive insurance dates back to the early 1950s. Subsequently, and until the mid-1990s, the number of captives in the world grew to more than 4,500.[8]

Captive insurance offers firms many advantages. Chief among them are that firms can keep the premium income within the family and control the risks. Compared with regular insurers, captive insurers enjoy lower administrative and operating costs and other overheads, which translate into a lower cost of coverage. Most important, captive insurers often wield significant bargaining power in the reinsurance market because they hold a large volume of contracts. This helps firms cut down on reinsurance costs. Some firms also prefer to deal directly in the reinsurance market because of its greater flexibility and risk tolerance. So setting up captive insurers was the way to go.

With all these advantages in mind, many multinational groups and conglomerates began to explore captive insurance. They were prodded along in the 1990s by the new government incentives to turn Hong Kong into a captive insurance centre.

In the Insurance Companies (Amendment) Ordinance 1997, effective 1 May 1997, a number of concessions were put in place. Table 6.4 indicates them.[9]

Table 6.4 Selected Requirements in 1997: General Business Insurer vs. Captive Insurer

Item	General Business Insurer	Captive Insurer
Minimum Capital Requirement:	HK$10 million	HK$2 million
Solvency Margin:	The greatest of: a. generally 20% of the relevant premium income; or b. generally 20% of the relevant claims outstanding; or c. HK$10 million The greatest of: a. 5% of the net premium income; or b. 5% of the net claims outstanding; or c. HK$2 million	To maintain assets in Hong Kong of an amount not less than 80% of its Hong Kong liabilities plus solvency margin
Valuation Regulation:	**Requirement for Assets in Hong Kong:** Assets and liabilities to be valued on statutory basis as prescribed by Valuation Regulation	Assets and liabilities to be valued on the basis of Generally Accepted Accounting Principles

Source: Insurance Company (Amendment) Ordinance 1997

The annual fees and authorization fees for a captive insurer together are $22,600, one-tenth of the fees paid by other authorized insurers. The IA, subject to the sufficiency of the information submitted, is committed to dealing with an application within two months.

At the time of Hong Kong's return to Chinese sovereignty, on 1 July 1997, the SAR was already ranked as a global player in terms of the number of insurance firms in operation. Among 215 firms, 151 were in general business, 45 in life, with the balance being composites. Of these, only 29 were authorized reinsurers. Slightly less than half of all firms were incorporated locally; the rest hailed from 27 countries; British firms, which numbered 25, accounted for the most from any one nation. Five of the top ten insurance giants had a branch in Hong Kong, a sure sign that the city met or surpassed international standards.

Chapter 7
The Development of Life Insurance and Bancassurance in the Post-Handover Decade

The global rise of bancassurance in the last thirty years had Hong Kong the international financial centre following the fad and catching up with the world. Over the past five years, Hong Kong's insurers formed strategic alliances with domestic banks to build up insurance sales pipelines and get a piece of the action. This set off a re-alignment of retail banking and a demand for financial planning services. This chain of events spurred on a diversification of the local insurance industry.

— *Insurance Professionals*, July 2002

The handover on 1 July 1997 made Hong Kong a Special Administrative Region (SAR) within China. Around that time, the provisional government set about adding seats in the Legislative Council to represent such specific industries and other 'functions', such as finance, insurance, real estate, and commerce; hence these members were representatives of 'functional constituencies'. On 24 March of the same year, the HKFI's special joint session submitted a proposal to the preparatory committee of the SAR government, pointing out that insurance has a crucial role in Hong Kong's financial market. The proposal also stressed that the sector already satisfied the four criteria used to designate functional constituencies in the SAR's first Legislative Council. The HKFI actively encouraged industry practitioners to register to vote and run for office.

Finally, in 1998, the HKFI was assigned the first-ever functional seat in the Legislative Council. Bernard Charnwut Chan, now president of the Asia Insurance Co. Ltd., won the election. At the time those vying for the seat included AIA's Deputy Managing Director Alex Wong; Union's General Manager Steven Lau, and National Mutual's Y. K. Chan.

Three Crises

(1) The impact of the financial crisis

A few months after the handover, Hong Kong was swept up in the region's much-noted financial crisis. Within a year the Hang Seng Index had plunged by 60%, from the 7 August 1997 high of 16,673 to the nadir of 6,600 on 13 August 1998. Property prices dropped by more than half, pushing many homeowners into negative equity territory. Beginning in

Fig. 7.1
Members of the HKFI's special joint session travel to Beijing to lobby for a functional seat on Hong Kong's Legislative Council, March 1996.

September 1997, the GDP slipped for five consecutive quarters. In 1998, the economy contracted by 5%, the worst performance since World War II.

Needless to say, the insurance sector suffered. Both premium revenues and income dropped precipitously. There was a surfeit of insurers, resulting in over-capacity and ruthless rate-cutting. In 1999, gross and net premium revenues decreased, respectively, by 8% and 9% from the previous year. The sector reported a loss of $1.38 billion.

But by 2000 the downturn had reversed. Gross and net premiums for general insurance showed growth of 7% and 9% respectively. But in March 2001, HIH Insurance Ltd. and its seventeen entities in Australia were ordered by the Australian government to liquidate. HIH's three subsidiaries in Hong Kong were taken into receivership by the OCI for failing to meet the capital requirement necessary for claims compensation.

In light of this, in early 2002 the OCI tightened the captive-insurance ceiling for all general insurers by limiting it to no more than 10% of the company's share capital.

(2) The impact of 9/11

On 11 September 2001, the twin towers of the World Trade Centre in New York were destroyed by two hijacked commercial airliners. It was an enormous blow to the general insurance sector globally. By some estimates, the industry suffered a loss of US$50 billion to US$70 billion worldwide; the bulk of the burden fell on re-insurers. Because most local insurers were not exposed to risk coverage in the United States, only five firms posted losses (totalling roughly $60 million) directly related to 9/11. The indirect impact on the local sector, however, was substantial. On the day following the catastrophe, stock prices for publicly traded insurers such as Manulife, Chinese Life, and Pacific Century all plunged by more than 20%, even though the latter two firms do not count the United States as their primary markets. A small Japanese-owned firm in Hong Kong sustained such heavy losses that it had to apply to the court for reorganization. The OCI took appropriate measures to shield its local assets.

Losses aside, 9/11 reshaped the global insurance sector in other significant ways. For one, many insurers no longer covered terrorism risks and at the same time also drastically raised premiums on political-risk coverage. The aviation industry was dealt the biggest blow of all. On the one hand, insurers demanded that airlines expand their coverage, but, on the other, capped the maximum claim per flight at US$50 million. Some insurers unilaterally cancelled coverage for political and terrorism risks for airline companies. All this threatened the viability of the airlines in case of an accident, because they would not receive adequate compensation to cover the losses. As a stop-gap measure, the U.S. Congress approved a bailout of US$18 billion to keep American carriers aloft.

The Hong Kong government took a similar tack. On 24 September 2001, the Legislative Council finance committee approved a motion to offer the three domestic airlines (Cathay Pacific, Dragonair, and Air Hong Kong), the Airport Authority, and all allied service providers third-party risk coverage pertaining to war, hijacking, and related hazards. The coverage, with a limit of $62 billion per incident, was good for one month. With this government backing, Cathay Pacific and Dragonair were able to reach an agreement with their insurers to cover war risks and pre-empt any service interruption. Ten days later, on 4 October, the Aviation Authority approved a surcharge of $10 to $47 per flight to be levied by fifteen airlines to cover war risks.

The retrenchment of terrorism risk coverage affected many segments of the insurance industry. From late 2001 to early 2002, many re-insurance contracts were successfully renewed only after coverage for terrorism was dropped. This set up a chain reaction that jeopardized even run-of-the-mill employees' compensation and motor policies. Most of these policies did not cover war risks but implicitly covered terrorism. But since re-insurers reneged on terrorism coverage, many such policies had to be revised.

By law, employers are required to take out comprehensive coverage for their workers, without which as many as three million workers may not legally report to their workplaces.

The withdrawal of terrorism coverage also threatened the legality of all existing motor vehicle (third-party risk) policies. Ultimately, the government came to the rescue by earmarking $10 billion for insurers to underwrite losses in cases of terrorist acts. Insurers were required to pay a 3% levy on their premium revenues to subscribe to this government-backed protection.

The 9/11 ripple effect did not stop there. Premium rates for cargo transport, tourism, accident, and other coverage all shot up. War coverage rates for cargo soared more than tenfold, while premiums for jewellery coverage also spiked up by several magnitudes. In about a year, rates for employees' compensation policies increased by anywhere from 20% to 175%.

To be sure, the terror attacks hammered home for the people of Hong Kong the fragility and the vagaries of life. Many turned to life coverage as a safeguard. In 2001, new life contracts (excluding retirement coverage) totalled $17 billion, a 48% increase from the year before.

(3) The impact of Severe Acute Respiratory Syndrome

In 2003, SARS ravaged Hong Kong, sickening more than 1,750 people to the point of hospitalization and killing 300. By the end of May 2003, the industry had satisfied nearly 500 SARS-related claims and paid out a total of $105 million. Needless to say, premium rates went up, especially for hospital and medical personnel. However, later that year, more than a dozen private hospitals were refused SARS coverage when they negotiated their insurance contracts. Some insurers even went so far as to express their desire to decline employees' compensation coverage for the medical field in the next year. This, of course, troubled not just the medical sector but also the public at large.

After much government effort, the insurance and medical sectors reached an agreement, with ten or so insurers stepping up to cover SARS. This came at a cost—of four to six times the prevailing premium.

Fig. 7.2
Severe Acute Respiratory Syndrome ravaged Hong Kong in 2003. By May, insurers had satisfied nearly 500 SARS-related claims and paid out a total of $105 million.

In the wake of SARS the general public's interest in medical coverage swelled, while more insurers were making liability coverage more affordable to doctors. By law, liability coverage was solely voluntary, so when uncovered doctors got sued for compensation they often had to pay out of their own pockets. Not a few went bankrupt as a result. Coverage was made available to both Western-trained doctors and practitioners of traditional Chinese medicine.

Following the 9/11 terrorist attacks and the SARS outbreak, the public voiced its concern about the lack of employees' compensation insurance coverage for certain high-risk trades. The HKFI responded by advocating an employees' compensation provision as a last resort for employers who could not otherwise secure coverage in the marketplace. An Employees' Compensation Insurance Residual Scheme Bureau was soon formed to take over administration of the residual scheme, with the HKFI serving as the administrator. Participation in the residual scheme was mandatory for all employees' compensation insurers, each bearing a slice of the accepted risk derived based on its market share.

Fig. 7.3
A ceremony marking the opening of the Employees' Compensation Insurance Residual Scheme Bureau, 18 April 2007.

The Development of Long-Term Insurance in the Post-Handover Decade

As previously noted, at the time of the 1997 handover Hong Kong had one of the world's highest concentrations of insurance companies per capita. However, the proportion of the population with life coverage, at 53%, still lagged behind that of the developed world. In Europe and North America, 80% of people had coverage; in Japan, 90%. Needless to say, the untapped local life market remained vast. The Mandatory Provident Fund that was then to be instituted by the government was a sure promise of more growth. Global insurers also saw Hong Kong as the future gateway to the mainland market, which China was required to open up as a member of the World Trade Organization.

Shortly after the financial crisis of 1997, the life market already achieved record growth. In 1999, new long-term policy sales clocked in at $11.4 billion, a 33.4% increase from the previous year. More than 60% of the increase came from life products. Part of the growth may have been encouraged by the government's decision in 1999 to eliminate the estate duty on all contracts denominated in Hong Kong dollars.

Finally—and it had been a long time coming—in February 2000 the government rolled out the Mandatory Provident Scheme and accepted applications from all those who were eligible. By October, all employees and employers were required to begin contributing to the scheme. The launch provided tremendous business opportunities for participating insurers. By some estimates, about $20 billion of the pension fund would be managed by either insurance firms or bank-affiliated trusts.

This also helped give insurers a solid footing to sell to new clients, especially those whose pension funds were managed by them. Meanwhile, some insurers resorted to more unconventional marketing, such as holding travelling exhibitions and carnivals to attract customers. Others appealed to clients by offering customized coverage, which allowed them to pick whatever risks against which they would like to be insured.

All in, the post-handover decade saw exponential growth in the life sector. From 2000 to 2007, non-linked personal-life premium income doubled, to $20.3 billion, while premium revenues for investment-linked life policies expanded by 12.5 times, to $60 billion. The top five firms took nearly 60% of the market, as Table 7.1 indicates.

Table 7.1 Top Five Life Insurers in Hong Kong, 2007

Insurer	Total Contract Value (in HK$bn)	Market Share (%)
Manulife	25.4	14.4
AIA	24.8	14.1
HSBC	24.7	14
Prudential	15.7	8.9
Hang Seng	9.5	5.4

Source: Hong Kong Commissioner of Insurance

Supervising Insurance Intermediaries: Review and Improvement

In post-handover Hong Kong, life products gained popularity, as did insurance agenting as a profession. In 1997, there were 31,200 agents; that figure jumped to 48,500 two years later, a 55% surge. During the same period, the number of life contracts rose from 3.4 million to nearly 5 million.

As products became increasingly sophisticated and the supervision process more complex, intermediaries needed to meet higher professional standards to protect policyholders' interest. With that in mind, in July 2001 the OCI published a consultation document, 'Review of Regulatory System for Insurance Intermediaries', which examined the self-regulatory system that had been in place since 30 June 1995 and in accordance with Part X of the Insurance Companies Ordinance (Cap. 41).

This was especially timely in light of the growing volume of complaints. From 1998 to 2000, the number of complaints lodged against agents and brokers more than doubled, from 208 to 459.

'There has been growing public concern over the professionalism and conduct of insurance intermediaries, as evidenced by the increasing number of complaints received,' the consultation document said. 'The aim of the review is to identify areas for improvement of the existing self-regulatory system.'

The document continued:

> ... since the [various] codes [of practice] are self-regulatory in nature, legal sanctions are not applicable for non-compliance and lacks legal backing. They do not specify requirements or good practice on certain major operations areas such as remittance of premiums and notification of claims; there is inadequate practical guidance to agents to ensure that relevant information is properly disclosed and explained to their clients; no effective measures in addressing the poaching of agents and replacement of polices among insurers.
>
> The two approved broker bodies, the Hong Kong Confederation of Insurance Brokers (CIB) and Professional Insurance Brokers Association Limited (PIBA), are not affiliated with each other, so inevitably there are some disparities in interpreting and implementing the requirements on admission and on-going supervision of members. . . . That fact that all their executive committee members come from broker companies also [reflects] an apparent lack of independence in performing their self-regulatory functions and presents a potential conflict of interest. . . . The existing regulations on brokers are relatively less stringent in Hong Kong. . . . The IA has limited sanction power over unethical conducts of broker members of the approved broker bodies.[1]

Fig. 7.4
A seminar organized by the Office of the Commissioner of Insurance, the Insurance Intermediaries Quality Assurance Scheme, 7 May 1999.

The review thus concluded that there was a need to tighten supervision of intermediaries, and to do so it suggested borrowing a strategy of the Securities & Futures Commission.

In Hong Kong, the 'Securities and Futures Bill' was gazetted on 24 November 2000 to provide for the regulatory framework for investment intermediaries. The SFC will conduct background vetting on their intermediaries to ensure that they are fit and proper. This background vetting procedure is currently not adopted by self-regulatory organizations in the licensing of insurance intermediaries. Besides with the proposed expansion of the definition of 'securities' to include 'interests in a collective investment scheme', insurers and insurance intermediaries dealing in or advising on insurance products that are interests in a collective investment scheme will fall within the regulatory regime of SFC and need to be licenses to do so. Insurers and insurance intermediaries will then be regulated by two regulatory authorities over their investment-linked long term business.

In January 2000, in its continuing efforts to raise professional standards among insurance intermediaries, the IA introduced the Insurance Intermediaries Quality Assurance Scheme to require insurance intermediaries to pass qualifying examinations. All insurance intermediaries, chief executives or responsible officers, and technical representatives were required to pass the test, the Insurance Intermediaries Qualifying Examination, which was conducted by the Vocational Training Council, to receive their licenses. The examination consisted of four papers, including a compulsory one on the principles and practice of insurance; the others were a qualifying paper each on general insurance, investment-linked long-term insurance, and long-term insurance. A separate paper for travel insurance agents was introduced in May 2006, as was, later on, one for agents offering products related to the Mandatory Provident Fund.

All practicing intermediaries had to pass the exams by the end of 2001 and be registered to conduct business. All those who entered the industry from 2000 onward were required not only to pass the exams but also to comply thereafter with the requirements of a continuing professional development programme. Fully 86% of practitioners passed the exams when the two-year transitional period ended on 31 December 2001 and obtained the licenses necessary to stay in business; there was an overall 47% passing rate for the papers. The qualifying exams, we can say without a doubt, served dramatically to improve the quality of intermediaries.

Peter Tam
Chief Executive, The Hong Kong Federation of Insurers
Joined the industry in 1990

Hongkongers are known globetrotters, so insurers are constantly trying various avenues to sell them on the importance of travel coverage. With such coverage, in event of accidents, policyholders are entitled to not only death, injury, and medical benefits but also emergency assistance. Still, many people shrugged that off. It wasn't until the Southeast Asia tsunami and the Egypt bus crash brought the inherent risks of travel close to home that many minds were changed.

I still remember getting the word on the bus crash as soon as I got up. It was on the third day of the Chinese New Year in 2006. A Hong Kong tour group had a serious accident in Hurghada, Egypt. Fourteen dead, nine injured. The HKFI immediately set up an ad hoc emergency committee. We called the Travel Industry Council of Hong Kong (TIC) and got the confirmation that all tour group members were covered by travel insurance. Next, we got in touch with the eight insurers who offered the coverage; two of them, through their international partners, dispatched a medical team to Hurghada within a few hours. The Cairo-based team spoke the local dialect and was great help. A Hong Kong team later arrived to stabilize some of the wounded.

On our end, there was a lot to be done within the first twenty-four hours. We set up a hotline to field the public's questions on insurance benefits and the progress on the rescue. We called a meeting with the tour company, the TIC, and all the insurers and emergency rescue service companies involved. We worked with the OCI, the Home Affairs Office, Immigration Department, and the Security Bureau in arranging for the wounded and the remains of the dead to come home.

Some of the more seriously wounded were diverted to Paris and Zurich for their more advanced medical infrastructure. Those with less severe injuries flew home in the company of family members or medical personnel. All of the remains arrived two days after the accident and the wounded came home within the week.

The aftermath of this tragedy—happening eight thousand miles away with considerable casualties—was proficiently handled through the seamless coordination of various industry parties and practitioners. This boosted Hong Kong people's confidence in travel-insurance coverage. The number of policyholders was on the rise ever since.

Industry Groups and Professional Organizations

As the sector continued to expand in the past decades, the ranks of practitioners swelled accordingly. Myriad industry groups and professional organizations therefore came into being.

(1) Trade groups of intermediaries

Among the intermediaries' groups, the Hong Kong Insurers' Club is the oldest. Back in the 1960s, social events for practitioners were few and far between. Yet, a smattering of expatriates and high-level local executives tended to socialize with each other privately. As such gatherings became a monthly routine they attracted more and more participants. Thus, in 1964, the Hong Kong Insurers' Club was formed, but it admitted only management-level practitioners. Formal luncheon seminars, not relaxing social activities, formed most of the club's programme. Membership was predominantly non-Chinese, and the lingua franca was English.

Feeling left out of the social circle, a dozen like-minded local practitioners founded the Chinese Underwriters Club (CUC) in 1976. The CUC's members met over informal dinners every other month and conversed primarily in Cantonese. Even so, the CUC started out with an air of exclusivity, limiting membership to a hundred. But the quota could not be maintained, given the number of practitioners clamouring to join. At its peak, the club boasted more than a 1,000 members. As of 2008, the membership exceeded 300, the majority being Chinese.

On 29 March 1973, the Hong Kong Life & Pension Society was founded with fifty-two members to focus on professional development and training as well as to establish and implement professional standards. The inaugural chairman, Y. K. Chan, recalled that at its founding, members were all passionate practitioners in the fledgling life sector. By July 1980 it was renamed the Life Underwriters Association of Hong Kong. As of 2010, it had around 8,500 members.

The Hong Kong Confederation of Insurance Brokers was formed by the merger, in 1993, of the Hong Kong Insurance Brokers Association and the Hong Kong Society of Insurance Brokers. Its formation was prompted by the government's desire to consult a more representative and unified brokers' group as it moved toward regulating their professional standards, according to Adrian King, the founding chairman. The confederation was active in submitting its input to the government's ordinance reform committee and the OCI. And when the amended Insurance Companies Ordinance went into effect in June 1995, its section empowered the confederation to devise self-regulatory measures.

Yet, another brokers' group, the Professional Insurance Brokers Association, was founded in January 1988, with twelve corporate members. But now it boasts more than 280 corporate members and 3,000 registered chief executives or company representatives. From the very beginning, the association has honed in on its members' professional ethics and conduct. Regular panels and special seminars were organized to enhance members' knowledge. These efforts paid off when the association got the government's nod to be the official body overseeing members' conduct.

And on 4 February 1994, after more than a year of ground work, the Hong Kong Chamber of Insurance Intermediaries (HKCII) was founded to represent agents and brokers serving life and general insurers. Inaugural chairman Gregory Fong explained that HKCII was established primarily to foster the collaborative spirit among insurance intermediaries with an eye toward ensuring fair competition. This, Fong hoped, would result in a win-win-win situation for customers, insurers and intermediaries. In 2010, the organization had 378 members.

The General Agents and Managers Association of Hong Kong (GAMA) was 'imported' from the United States in 1994 to be the city's only organization of life agents. Its mission is to raise management skills, such as in recruiting, training, supervision, and workforce motivation. Every year, GAMA would organize conferences, bringing together industry veterans as well as outsiders to share their wisdom and experience and thus raising the industry's profile. In 2006, a professional development centre was established to enhance teaching and research in the life sector as well as related qualifications in financial management. Within the first few months of its founding, the local GAMA became the overseas branch that boasted the most members under the U.S. umbrella organization.

The Hong Kong General Insurance Agents Association was founded in 1997 to represent the interest of general agents. With roughly a hundred members at its founding, the association saw its membership dwindle to eighty by 2010, due to a decrease in the general number of insurance agents.

Later, the Hong Kong Insurance Practitioners General Union was established, in January 2003, to resolve the grievances of brokers, agents, and salaried professionals. With its emphasis on solidarity, justice, and professionalism, the union purports to fight for its members' rights to fair treatment.

(2) Professional associations

Besides the trade groups for intermediaries, the sector also has a number of professional associations. The oldest among them is the Insurance Institute of Hong Kong (IIHK). Founded in 1967, the IIHK is known for its role in raising professional standards within the sector and competitiveness amongst practitioners. Through the years, the institute has organized training courses and specialized seminars for its members.

Formed in 1967, the Actuarial Association of Hong Kong began with five members. In 1972, Peter Luk became the first local actuary and Fellow of the Institute of Actuaries of English (FIA), and Che Lam was made a Fellow of the Society of Actuaries of the United States of America. Three others followed in Luk's footsteps by the late 1970s.

Renamed the Actuarial Society of Hong Kong in 1994, it brought in more members beyond the insurance sector, from consultancies, finance and investment firms, the government, and educational institutions. Still, the sector accounted for nearly 70% of the membership. By 2010, the society had more than 750 members on its rolls.

The LOMA Society of Hong Kong was formed in 1978 by a handful of insurance executives who had been made Fellows of the Life Management Institute (FLMI). When the FLMI examinations were first introduced in Hong Kong, in 1970, only fifteen sat for them. But now at least several hundred people, most of them working in the back office or in administrative positions at insurance firms, will take the examinations every time they are offered.

The Hong Kong Society of Certified Insurance Practitioners was established in August 1998 and began admitting members with five or more years of management experience. All of its members obtained their professional qualifications in Britain, the U.S., Australia, or other foreign countries.

The Institute of Financial Planners of Hong Kong was formed in June 2000 to maintain high professional standards and self-discipline for the city's providers of financial planning services. In November 2000, the institute achieved its first milestone when it was approved by the Financial Planning Standards Board to offer testing and certification for the Certified Financial Planner in Hong Kong and Macau. The institute now boasts more than 10,000 members.

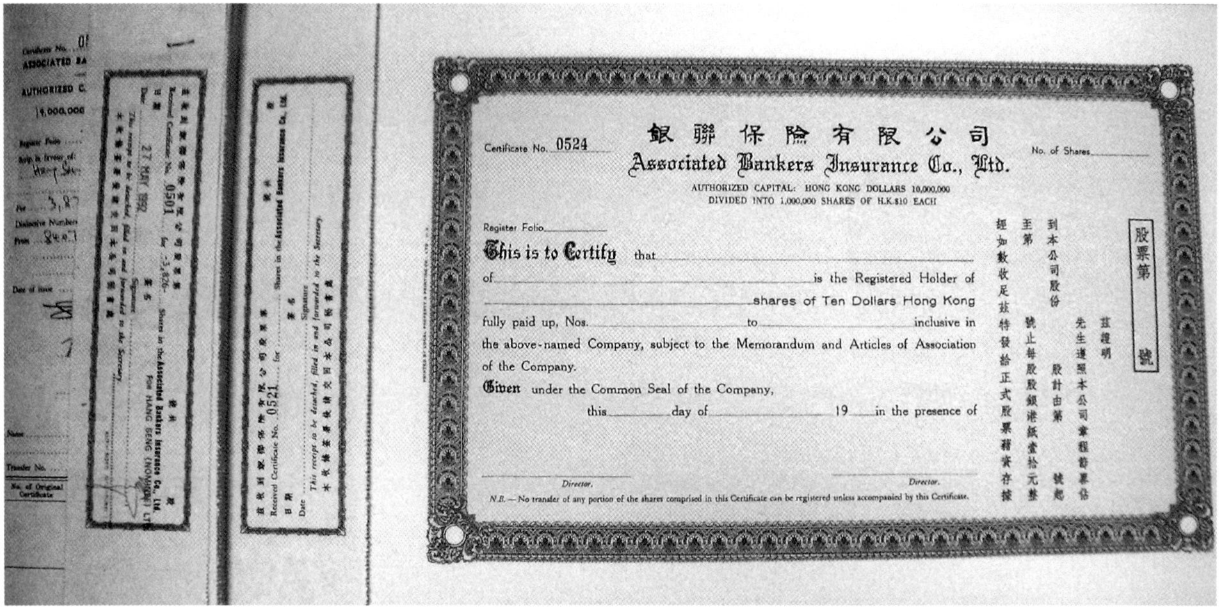
Certificate No. 0524

銀聯保險有限公司

Associated Bankers Insurance Co., Ltd.

AUTHORIZED CAPITAL: HONG KONG DOLLARS 10,000,000
DIVIDED INTO 1,000,000 SHARES OF H.K.$10 EACH

No. of Shares

股票第 號

Register Folio

This is to Certify that
of is the Registered Holder of
shares of Ten Dollars Hong Kong
fully paid up, Nos. to inclusive in
the above-named Company, subject to the Memorandum and Articles of Association
of the Company.
Given under the Common Seal of the Company,
this day of 19 in the presence of

Director. Director.

N.B.—No transfer of any portion of the shares comprised in this Certificate can be registered unless accompanied by this Certificate.

Fig. 7.5
A stock certificate issued by Associated Bankers Insurance Co. Ltd., a bancassurance company led by Hang Seng Bank.

The Rise of Bancassurance

For the longest time conventional insurers have prided themselves on offering personalized, comprehensive service one-to-one through both the agency system and their own sales networks. But as banking expanded globally with more value-added services, bancassurance rode high on this global expansion.

However, bancassurance has become more prevalent and popular only over the last three decades. Beginning in the 1980s, most banks in Europe were firmly in the insurance marketing business. In Britain alone, from 1992 to 1996, bancassurance's market share more than doubled, from 7% to 15%, at an average annual rate of 21%.

Bancassurance is marketed in various ways: either by the bank or the insurer taking the lead, or through concerted efforts of the bank and the insurer together. When an insurer takes the lead, it analyzes the database of the bank's clientele and tailors products and marketing strategies based on the composite statistics resulting from such analysis. The most commonly marketed products are term life and accident. When a bank takes the lead, it uses the partnering bank's sale force to sell clients on various types of insurance products. In this case, a financial consultant with an intermediary's license conducts a comprehensive analysis of clients on their financial planning and recommends certain investment and insurance products for their portfolios.

The development of bancassurance in Hong Kong can be traced to the Associated Bankers Insurance Co. Ltd. in the 1960s and CIGNA in the 1970s. In 1965, Hang Seng Bank started Associated, with Wing Hang Bank, Wing Lung Bank, and Bank of East Asia banks as shareholders. That arguably was the first bancassurance venture in Hong Kong, with a bank taking the lead. But CIGNA, also, was a bancasssurance pioneer. In 1979, CIGNA partnered with banks and credit card companies to market its insurance products, through both direct mailing and telemarketing. Yet, the heyday of bancassurance would not come until the mid-to-late 1990s.

When the financial crisis hit in July 1997, the real estate bubble burst and interest rates stayed high. All this took huge bites out of banks' margins. As banks looked for revenue sources other than interest, bancassurance presented new opportunities for income streams. So large and medium-sized banks tapped into their vast client networks and menus of professional services to expand into the sector, either through their own insurance subsidiaries or by partnering insurers.

The greatest advantages enjoyed by bancassurance are a bank's access to a vast client database and a network of branches. The most popular marketing tactic has been

Fig. 7.6
A dragon dance at the opening ceremony of the Prudential Assurance Co.'s offices in Tsim Sha Tsui, 19 May 2000.

through client contact at the branch level. A bank's customers are invited to attend bank-sponsored events such as investment seminars, informational sessions on new products and mutual funds, and so on. Through these gatherings, a bank's financial consultants can maximize their contact with the customers and 'soft sell' insurance products. This has proved far more effective than traditional hard selling because customers tend to have faith in a bank's institutionalized, standardized financial planning service.

Some examples of the myriad of bancassurance products are as follows:

- Mortgage insurance, such as the residential-mortgage protection plan offered by Standard Chartered. Under the plan, if policyholders become unable to make mortgage payments due to involuntary unemployment or short-term disabilities, they are entitled to up to $200,000 or six months' coverage.

- Credit card–related life products. AIA and Citibank jointly promoted a plan that granted holders of certain credit cards up to $100,000 in automatic life coverage

- Products related to the Mandatory Provident Fund. These are available at all HSBC and Hang Seng Bank branches. The Bank of China also joined with Prudential in offering such products.

Of the major banking groups, HSBC Life Holdings, part of the HSBC Group, fared best in bancassurance. Founded in 1976, HSBC Life tapped into the banking giant's client pool as early as in 1993. But the biggest growth did not surface until after 1997.

C. F. Choy
CEO, The Bank of China Group Life Assurance Co. Ltd.
Joined the industry in 1982

I was assigned to the insurance department when I first joined the HSBC Group, and thus began my life-time affair with bancassurance. In those early days, bancassurance's growth remained rather straitjacketed. That's because retail banking was already hugely successful and lucrative, so there's a lack of incentive to blaze the bancassurance trail. I remember a veteran banker saying this to me: 'I don't know what on earth you fellows in the insurance department are toiling for. Whenever we bankers sign a contract, it's at least for a few million dollars. But you guys' policies make only a few hundred dollars a pop. It's peanuts.'

Figs. 7.7–7.9
Advertising brochures of leading insurers, 2000s.

For me, the idea of banassurance is simple; it boils down to understanding your clients' needs. We used the financial-planning approach and took a comprehensive look at a client's portfolios and asset-management goals. So then we can recommend the appropriate share that goes into savings, investment, insurance, etc. The bottom line is everybody needs some coverage; the trick is to figure out how much a client can afford. That way you can make sure you sell the right policy and thus minimize cancellations and losses on the client's part.

Effective bancassurance marketing calls for integration—of the computer system, back office personnel, client database, etc. For instance, when a bank customer comes to the counter for currency exchange, the teller should follow up by asking if the customer might want to take out travel insurance.

Whether bancassurance has been a success in Hong Kong remains to be seen. But remember that veteran banker who once shrugged off bancassurance as peanuts? After he'd retired he joined the board of directors of a bancassurance firm. That tells you something about the growing clout of bancassurance.

The Rise of the Niche Market

As the sector grew mature, competition in the mainstream market intensified. To boost premium income and expand the client base, insurers clamoured to explore the niche markets. This resulted in a flowering of new policy types.

In contrast to conventional products such as employees' compensation, motor vehicle, and travel insurance, the niche market caters to individual needs for coverage from horses and collectibles to jewellery and yachts.

The rise of the niche market was prompted by the increased competition from banks. As bancassurance gained market share in the conventional market, insurers looked for other revenues elsewhere and increasingly invested in the niche market, according to Geoffrey Lung, a veteran practitioner. Also, relentless mergers and acquisitions among global players have brought specialty know-how to bear in the local insurance market and made it possible to expand into the niche market. Equine insurance is one such example.

Insuring horses was no novelty, because it is as old as the racing franchise in Hong Kong. For many years Lloyd's has been the go-to place for equine insurance. Beginning in the 1970s, large agencies such as Mollers' began to act as intermediaries for purebred coverage. Even some local insurers have increasingly warmed to the equine line in recent years. Of the 1,400 horses currently in the stable, about 800 have some kind of coverage for death or loss of racing capability. When horses are shipped to the city from overseas, such as from Australia and New Zealand, they also have to have transit coverage. Lloyd's coverholder is the one-stop shop for coverage.

Another product gaining popularity is one covering private collections. The scope of such coverage can be very broad. It usually covers the more common collectibles, including antiques, postage stamps, artworks, and timepieces, but it can include items deemed valuable by a collector, for example, commemorative badges, feather fans, red wines, personal letters, Ming- or Qing-style furniture, and so on. Since most of these items carry no objective price tag, the coverage amount is either determined by professional evaluators or hashed out over discussions between the owner and the insurer.

Jewellery coverage also was getting noticed by the insurers. In the crime-riddled 1990s, insurers often were hit with losses covering jewellery. But as jewellery shops are equipped with advanced anti-theft systems and the Hong Kong Police keep a better pulse on local and global crime intelligence, robbers have a tougher time in their fencing operations.

As both the costs and risks associated with robberies rose, the number of cases dropped precipitously. Insurers now face significantly lower risks in covering jewellery. In addition to the domestic market, the city also exports stones to Europe and North America. So insurers should provide both retail coverage and transit coverage.

The emergence of other non-mainstream products was intricately linked to the rise of certain economic activities. As Hong Kong has hosted various international and domestic conferences in recent years, conference-cancellation products became a hit. Also, the rapid growth of the advertising sector gave rise to liability products that cover injuries incurred during the production of commercials.

The Development of Chinese-Owned Firms in Hong Kong

For the longest time, Hong Kong's insurance sector has been dominated by foreign firms, especially American and British insurers. That said, Chinese-owned firms have carved out a significant slice of the market. These include the pre–World War II establishments Sincere and Wing On and such postwar upstarts as Ming An, Associated Bankers, and Asia Insurance. But it was not until 1990s that the Chinese-owned firms emerged as a moneyed force to be reckoned with. Below are some of the major mainland players in the Hong Kong insurance sector:

China Taiping Insurance (HK) Co. Limited (formerly known as 'The Ming An Insurance Co. (HK) Ltd')

Ming An's forerunner was Shanghai's Ming An Property & Product Insurance. In 1949, The China Taiping Insurance (HK) Co. Limited (China Taiping) was incorporated in the territory with a registered capital of $1 million and paid-up capital of half as much. In its early years, its mainstays were mostly cargo, hull, and transport-liability products. During the 1960s, changing with the times, it switched gears and expanded its offerings in fire, employees' compensation, and, later, construction all-risks. It also served as agent for the Legal & General Assurance Society Ltd., a British company.

By the 1970s, China Taiping had jumped on the re-insurance bandwagon and took part in a joint venture with Jardine Matheson, HSBC, and the Bowring Group of London called the East Point Re-insurance Co. of Hong Kong Ltd. In the following decade, Ming An joined forces with the China Taiping Insurance (HK) Co. Ltd. and the People's Insurance Co. of China (Hong Kong) Ltd. to found the China Reinsurance (HK) Co. Ltd.

The Ming An (Holdings) Co. Ltd., the holding company of China Taiping, was listed on the main board of the Hong Kong Stock Exchange on 22 December 2006. Ming An Holdings became a wholly owned subsidiary of China Taiping Insurance Holdings Co. Ltd. (CTIH) and withdrew the listing of the company's shares on the exchange on 2 November 2009.

A year-to-year increase of 46% in gross written premiums, to $1.97 billion in 2008, placed China Taiping among the major general insurance companies in Hong Kong.

> *K. C. Hong*
> *Director, China Taiping Insurance (HK) Company Limited*
> *Joined the industry in 1951*
>
> *During the heyday of light industries, insurers devised many peculiar ways to calculate fire premiums. At that time it was common to find textiles and plastics factories under the same roof of an industrial building. However, since fire risks were quite a bit higher for plastics, even owners of textiles factories had to pay the higher premiums if they were housed in the same building. Also, the higher up the factories were the higher the premiums, especially when the factories were located on or above the fifteenth floor. That was because fire engines had ladders that could not reach farther up than the fifteenth floor.*

Taiping Reinsurance Co. Ltd. (formerly known as 'The China International Reinsurance Co Ltd')

Its first incarnation, as the Taiping Reinsurance Co. Ltd. (TPRe), was established in September 1980 by People's Insurance (a 40% stake), Ming An (30%), and China Taiping (30%).

By 1998, TPRe had already captured nearly 21% of the city's re-insurance premiums, making it the second largest such firm in the market, after Munich Re.

Later, in a 1999 restructuring, China Taiping Insurance Holdings Company Limited (CTIH) (formerly known as China Insurance International Holdings Company Limited) was set up and inherited all life business developed by the former China Reinsurance Co. since 1996. The business scope covered a wide range of products including life, health, and accident.

In 2000, the new holding company publicly listed its re-insurance subsidiary, the Taiping Reinsurance Co., Ltd. (TPRe) China International Re-insurance Co., as well as its re-insurance brokerage firm, Sino-Re, on the Hong Kong Stock Exchange. China Insurance thus became the first mainland insurance company to be publicly listed across the border. In 2008, the company achieved total premiums of RMB 6.6 billion and total assets RMB 17.4 billion.

The Bank of China Group

Bank of China Group Insurance was established in July 1992 and conducts business through six branches and two subsidiaries, the Bank of China Insurance Co. Ltd. and BOCG Life.

The former provides a wide range of general services, ranging from accident and health, motor, cargo in transit, and property to general liability and other products. The latter offers long-term life insurance products, including traditional and linked individual life insurance and group life insurance products through the Bank of China (Hong Kong)'s distribution network. By the end of 2005, BOCG Insurance's total consolidated assets were valued at $13 billion.

In 2005, the Shenzhen branch of BOCG Insurance completed a restructuring and was incorporated as a wholly owned subsidiary of BOCG Insurance, the Bank of China Insurance Co. Ltd. In December of the same year, the Bank of China Insurance Co. Ltd. received approval from the China Insurance Regulatory Commission to open its first domestic branch in Jiangsu Province.

In 2004, BOCG Insurance had consolidated gross written premiums of HK$3.8 billion and consolidated pre-tax profit of $265.5 million. Its net written premiums for its property and casualty insurance business ranked first in Hong Kong for seven consecutive years, from 1998 to 2004, according to OCI data.

As of year end 2005, BOCG Life had gross written premiums of HK$3,639 million. In April 2006, BOCG Insurance conditionally agreed to sell 51% of its interests in BOCG Life to Bank of China (Hong Kong) Holdings.

The Asia Insurance Co. Ltd. and Hong Kong Life Insurance

Among Chinese-owned firms, the Asia Insurance Co. is one of the oldest and most ambitious in the sector. In 1959, Bangkok Bank's Thai Chinese founder, Chin Sophonpanich, along with other prominent Chinese business executives, established what would become the region's leading general insurer and got it listed on the city's four stock exchanges in 1972.

Even at its listing, Asia Insurance had amassed $10 million in capital. The company would soon get two more shots in the arm. The Continental Group of USA, holding company of Diners Club, became a shareholder in 1976, followed by Chiyoda Fire & Marine Insurance of Japan in 1989. By 2007, Asia Insurance had obtained a Standard & Poor's 'A' rating.

In terms of business development, Asia Insurance has also been active in forming a number of joint ventures with partners around the region. The general insurer opened branches in Taiwan and Macau in the early 1980s. In 2001, Hong Kong Life Insurance was formed with other local financial institutions to offer comprehensive life insurance services.

In 2005, along with People's Insurance, Bangkok Bank, and the Sumitomo Life Insurance Co. of Japan, Asia Financial, under the leadership of Robin Chan and Bernard Charnwut

Fig. 7.10
The opening ceremony and press conference of Hong Kong Life, 23 April 2001.

Chan, started a joint venture to form PICC Life Insurance with a nationwide license to begin providing life insurance on the Mainland.

By 2006, the annual gross premiums of Asia Insurance put it in fifth place among local general insurers.

The Development of the Mainland Market

Throughout the 1990s, as the mainland's insurance market developed rapidly, efforts by Hong Kong insurers to tap into the mainland market grew apace.

Fig. 7.11
Ma Yongwei, chairman of the China Insurance Regulatory Commission, executes calligraphy to celebrate the opening of the HKFI's new headquarters at Wan Chai, 10 May 2001.

After the Insurance Law of the People's Republic of China (a.k.a. the Insurance Company Administration Provisions) was promulgated in 1995 and the Administrative Rule of Insurance Agents (a.k.a. the Provisional Regulations on the Control of Insurance) in 1996, China, in 1998, established its first-ever insurance regulatory commission, the China Insurance Regulatory Commission, a milestone in the development of an insurance sector with enormous potential. Since the handover, the economic tie that binds the Hong Kong and mainland insurance sectors has only tightened.

This culminated in the Mainland and Hong Kong Closer Economic Partnership Arrangement (CEPA), which was signed on 29 June 2003. It is the first free trade agreement between the Mainland and SAR. Under it, Hong Kong insurers are accorded the following significant concessions:

- Groups formed by Hong Kong insurance companies through re-grouping and strategic mergers are permitted to enter the mainland market subject to certain established market-access conditions;
- A maximum limit of capital participation by a Hong Kong insurance concern in a mainland insurance company is set at 24.9%;
- Hong Kong residents with insurance qualifications are permitted to work in the mainland insurance industry;
- Hong Kong insurance agencies are permitted to set up wholly owned companies on the Mainland to offer insurance agency services to mainland insurers.

For other foreign insurers, China's accession to World Trade Organization in 2001 required it to take steps to relax or even dismantle numerous market barriers. Foreign firms had previously been rare, and rare it was for such a firm—AIG, for instance—to make headway in the mainland market. Others could enter only by way of joint ventures with mainland firms.

For instance, in 1996, Manulife Financial's joint venture in Shanghai, the Zhong Hong Life Insurance Co. Ltd., became China's first joint venture life insurance company. Manulife-Sinochem is a joint venture company between Manulife (International) Ltd. (51% ownership) and the China Foreign Economic & Trade Trust & Investment Co., a member of the Sinochem group (49% ownership). By the end of 2007, the insurance regulatory commission had approved seven foreign insurers and five Chinese-foreign joint ventures.

In 2002, after its accession to the WTO, China enacted its Regulations for the Administration of Foreign-Invested Insurance Companies to fulfill its commitment to let in more foreign investors, not least insurers. To meet its WTO obligations, in December 2004, China 'lifted its previous restrictions limiting foreign insurers to fifteen cities and prohibiting the sale of group policies'.[2] For foreign insurers, China's 'potential for growth is immense, as less than 4% of China's 1.3 billion people have insurance'.[3] It also is a market full of challenges.

Yet, few Hong Kong–based heavyweights were deterred. In October 2002, HSBC Insurance Holdings Ltd. bought a 10% stake in the Ping An Insurance Co. of China Ltd. for US$600 million. At the time, that was the largest ever infusion of foreign capital in the Mainland's financial sector. By August 2005, HSBC doubled its Ping An stake to 19.9%. In the meantime, HSBC Insurance Brokers Ltd. entered into a joint venture agreement to offer insurance-broking and risk-management services to domestic and international clients on the Mainland, making it the first foreign joint venture there to have obtained an insurance-broking license to offer services to domestic customers. Also, HSBC partnered with Hua Yu Asset Management Ltd. in Shanghai and the Beijing Zhong Ke Engineering Co. to form HSBC Insurance Brokers Ltd., with headquarters in Beijing. With an injection of US$498,000, HSBC held a 24.9% stake in the new brokerage.

This new concern, licensed to undertake insurance broking, claims handling, re-insurance, and risk-management risk-consulting services, would focus on brokering large commercial risks, re-insurance business, international marine, aviation, transport, and health-care insurance to foreign investment entities. With it, HSBC's full-on plans for the mainland market were complete.

HSBC's Group Chairman, Sir John Bond, said in 2005, 'We are optimistic about the long term prospects of the insurance industry in mainland China.'[4]

In 2005, together with Bangkok Bank and Japan's Sumitomo Life Insurance, the Hong Kong–based Asia Financial Holdings partnered with PICC Holdings to form a joint venture.[5] The frenzy over the Mainland is best summed up by a top executive at TPRe (formerly known as "China International Re"): 'In the post-handover decade, Hong Kong insurers, no matter general or life, have seized the opportunity to expand', Chief Executive Officer Kenneth Ng said. 'Nearly eight of the top ten focus their attention squarely on the Mainland, in any shape and form and to differing degrees.'

Agnes Koon
Chief Executive, KSY Specialty Ltd., 2008–2009
Chairman of the Hong Kong Federation of Insurers

'HKFI' stands for more than the Hong Kong Federation of Insurers. A trademark of professionalism and dedication to consumer protection, it symbolizes our member corporations working together to promote the common interests of the industry and the public.

At its twentieth anniversary, HKFI is given a brand new look, which captures the essence of both the association's longstanding corporate identity as well as the core values of insurance. The focus of the new logo is the last letter, 'I'. With a bright red dot set against the navy blue, it sends out a clear message of insurance forming an integral part of all socio-economic activities. Portrayed as a torch with blazing flames, the letter carries a significant symbolic meaning.

Conclusion

Future Prospects of Hong Kong's Insurance Industry

> The insurance industry under the strong contribution from the life sector has achieved tremendous growth over the past twenty years. The annual premiums from both general and life insurance have increased fifteen times from $13 billion in 1988 to over $200 billion in 2007, now representing over 10% of the Hong Kong gross domestic product. The importance and value of insurance are now being recognized by the community. The industry provides risk and wealth management, appropriate protection and quality insurance solution to Hong Kong whether they are individual or groups, commercial, industrial SMEs or corporations.
>
> Insurance has become a vital pillar of Hong Kong's financial service industry and a major economic sector employing more than 100,000 people. The HKFI, as a trade association representing 136 insurers, is proud to see its mission of promoting insurance making significant progress over the years.
>
> While our industry prospers and thrives, we have never deviated from our firm commitment to actively practicing self-regulation.
>
> — Agnes Koon, *The Story of The Hong Kong Federation of Insurers*

The Insurance Sector's Contribution to the Economy

The reform and opening up of China in the 1980s set off a rapid transformation of Hong Kong's economy. Where manufacturing had once been king, the services sector became dominant. In 2007, manufacturing accounted for a mere 2.5% of GDP (as opposed to 70% in 1970), while services in 2007 accounted for 92.3% of the economy. Within the sector, finance, insurance, real estate, and business services were the most important producers, delivering 29% of GDP.

In 2008, the insurance sector generated $188 billion in gross premiums, amounting to about 12% of GDP, and it employed 46,000 people, 1.3% of the SAR's workforce.[1]

As a pillar of the financial services sector, the insurance industry offers long-term, general, and comprehensive products. From 1982 to 2007, Hong Kong's GDP expanded by 7.2 times, whereas gross premiums over the same period grew by 42 times. The penetration rate, meanwhile, grew from 2.5% to 13.6%, a spectacular surge.

The Basic Characteristics of Hong Kong's Insurance Industry

(1) A plethora of insurers and concentration of market share

At the moment, Hong Kong is one of the most liberalized and saturated insurance markets in the Asia-Pacific region—and, indeed, in the world. As of July 2010, Hong Kong had 170 authorized insurance companies, with 104 in general business, 46 in long-term, and the balance in composite. Fully 88 insurers are registered domestically, with the remainder in 22 different nations. Bermuda, Britain, and the United States are the most popular countries of incorporation, accounting for more than a quarter of all registrants.

Meanwhile, there is a high level of concentration in market share. Take the life market as an example. In 2007, the ten largest life insurers in Hong Kong took up 74% of the market, leaving the balance for thirty-seven insurers to carve up. As a rule, insurance companies compete on prowess of capital and reputation, so the nature of the business naturally favours the behemoths. But the large number of small to medium-sized insurers in Hong Kong means that there was room for survival as smaller fish in the pond, but only for so long.

As the government raised the bar for new entrants in the 1980s and as industry players were reshuffled by the global M&A mania of the 1990s, it became a game of survival of the fittest. The number of insurers in Hong Kong thus began to dwindle.

(2) High density and penetration

In 2007, the density of insurance in Hong Kong was US$3,373.3. That ranked the city No. 1 in Asia and No. 13 worldwide. And with a penetration rate of 11.8%, Hong Kong ranked No. 3 in Asia and No. 16 worldwide. ('Density' is the average insurance premium per capita; 'penetration rate' is the ratio of total premiums to GDP.)

Many international insurers also have ventured into the Hong Kong market since the handover. During the first post-handover decade, total gross premiums for the industry as a whole nearly tripled, from $52 billion to $188 billion in 2008.

(3) The life market rules

Since the mid-1980s, as factories headed north en masse and the services sector took off, the impact on the insurance market has been enormous. Demand for marine, fire, and employees' compensation products fell off a cliff, while the market for life products surged. By some estimates, premium income for general business rose 6% from 2004 to 2008, while premium income for life skyrocketed by 65%, from $98.4 billion to $162 billion, during the same period.

(4) Investment-linked products raise risks

The Mandatory Provident Scheme launched by the government in 2000 unleashed a rush of hot money into the stock market and a flood of public interest in investment-linked insurance products. As the financial meltdown of 2008 has shown, the risks associated with many of these derivative products were ill understood, even by investment professionals.

The conundrum for insurers of how to strike a balance between product innovation and policyholder protection remains.

(5) Dual supervision

Hong Kong's insurance sector is one of the few in the world that operates primarily on a self-regulatory basis, complemented with some degree of government supervision. Professional standards for practitioners are consistently raised to safeguard policyholders' interest. In 1990, the government broke its *laissez faire* mold and set up the Office of the Commissioner of Insurance to extend its supervision over the industry.

More recently, in 2009, a policyholders' protection fund was proposed to enhance protection for policyholders in the event of an insurer's insolvency, to help bolster public confidence in the insurance industry, and to promote the general stability of the insurance market. The proposal is currently under consultation.

This dual supervision system has its pros and cons. The obvious advantage is that the relationship between government regulators and practitioners is based on trust and transparency. This maximizes freedom and helps cut down the cost of doing business. The problem is that at times it is unclear who is, indeed, policing the industry.

Johnny Chen
CEO, Greater China/Southeast Asia, the Zurich Insurance Co. Ltd.
Joined the industry in 2005.

Hongkongers the ultimate risk-takers: Hong Kong policyholders don't give a damn about the protection value of life contracts; all they care about are the savings and investment yield. And they demand high returns for the high risks they dare to bear. So it's not a surprise to see that the first life policy for local policyholders is linked to high-risk investment options. They're more preoccupied with short-term returns and less concerned about future protection.

But after the baptism of fire that was the financial tsunami of 2008, I believe that insurers and policyholders alike are keen to go back to the basics, preferring products that guarantee savings and protection, albeit with lower returns.

The Hong Kong edge: The high penetration of insurance coverage has much to do with the city's sound legal system. Hong Kong is an international city that employs a good chunk of the footloose global workforce. But these migratory workers, either here for the long haul or on short-term assignments, tend to choose to take out a life policy here and keep it long after they've returned home—all because they have faith in the legal and insurance system here.

Looking Ahead

Hong Kong's insurance sector has weathered the ups and downs of more than a century and can boast an impressive record of development. New developments in 2009, namely the new requirements of Merchant Shipping (local vessels) (Compulsory Third Party Risks) Insurance and Building Management (Third Party Risks) Insurance, will serve only to further growth.

To be sure, teamwork and network management are just as crucial to future growth. Victor Fung, chairman of Li & Fung Ltd. and a world-famous proponent of supply-chain management, once wrote: 'Executives of insurance enterprises are becoming aware that successful coordination, integration, and management of key business processes across members of their supply chains will ultimately determine their competitive success. Insurance intermediaries/brokers increasingly realize that they no longer compete as solely autonomous entities. Instead, competition occurs more and more among entire supply chains. And they also know that they cannot produce an overall insurance solution without addressing the entire supply chain of their customers.'[2]

In November 2002, the Hong Kong government's Census and Statistics Department released the Thematic Household Survey Report No. 9, part of which includes a survey on insurance needs and opinions on insurance services. According to the survey, 'over half (52%) of the persons who had purchased insurance policies before indicated that they were quite satisfied/very satisfied with the insurance services received while 4.6% indicated that they were quite dissatisfied/very dissatisfied. Another 43.3% gave an average rating'.[3] And at the same time, 'the percentage of persons aged 18 and over who had purchased their own life insurance policies increased with educational attainment. The respective percentages were 55.9% for persons with tertiary educational attainment; and 43.3% for those with secondary/matriculation educational attainment'.[4]

It is evident from the survey that Hong Kong people at large hold a positive view of the industry and that their demand for products rises as they become more educated. All this bodes well for future development, especially in the life sector.

(1) Room for growth in private medical insurance

Most people in Hong Kong rely on the public health care system, which is funded mostly by taxpayers but heavily subsidized by government dollars. The services are very affordable, compared with private health care, and of high quality. However, private health care remains too expensive even for the middle class, so more and more increasingly seek out private medical insurance.

Meanwhile, as the public system is overloaded and costs shoot up, the government also has been exploring various schemes to encourage more people to take out medical coverage to pay for private care. Between late 2009 and early 2010, the government held two rounds of public consultation to solicit views on shoring up healthcare financing and mandating health insurance coverage.

In a February 2010 survey conducted by The Chinese University of Hong Kong which was based on a sample of 1,013 full-time employees, an overwhelming 80 percent of respondents supported a tax deduction for private medical insurance policyholders, and as much as one-third of those polled said this kind of deduction would entice them to buy medical insurance and rely less heavily on public health care. However, more than half were adamantly against any sort of mandatory medical savings scheme proposal, akin to the current mandatory scheme for retirement savings.

If the government implements a plan to offer substantial and meaningful financial incentives for more people to buy into medical coverage, this will portend a tremendous growth potential for the industry.

Mike Lee
Vice President, Operations, MassMutual Asia Ltd.
Joined the industry in 1986

The AIDS scare: Sometime around the late 1980s, more and more people came to recognize an incurable disease called AIDS. Because AIDS was highly infectious and at that time killing most of those who were infected, insurance companies got very nervous. So the HKFI quickly stepped up to the plate with a raft of recommendations. One of the most important was a provision subjecting all policyholders with US$250,000 or more in coverage to an HIV test. This really has helped the sector contain the risks of covering AIDS.

(2) The emerging mainland market

Industry practitioners have been eyeing the huge mainland market and its rising living standards and, hence, demand. On 29 June 2003, the central government in Beijing and the Hong Kong SAR government signed off on the Closer Economic Partnership Arrangement (CEPA), their first free-trade agreement. Effective on 1 January 2004, the CEPA waives all customs taxes on Hong Kong goods shipped to the Mainland and permits all locally registered insurance companies to 'form strategic partnerships in order to enter the mainland insurance market subject to certain established market-access conditions' and 'all Hong Kong residents with insurance qualifications to work in the mainland's sector'. In one of the five CEPA supplements, permission was given for insurance intermediaries to attain mainland qualifications by sitting for examinations in Hong Kong and for Hong Kong agencies to set up wholly owned companies on the Mainland to provide agency services to mainland insurance companies.

Furthermore, the Hong Kong Monetary Authority (HKMA) and the People's Bank of China jointly agreed in July 2010 to lift the limit on Hong Kong residents' purchase of yuan-denominated wealth management products. This promised to open up the yuan-denominated markets on Hong Kong insurers. Already, the Life Insurance Council's Renminbi Life Insurance Products Working Group has completed its proposal to launch annuities and other life products in the Mainland, pending further discussion with both HKMA and the OCI.

Another important development concerns the release of the Outline of the Plan for the Reform and Development of the Pearl River Delta (2008–2020) by the Beijing government's National Development and Reform Commission.

Its significance lies in the fact that for the first time, the central government folded Hong Kong and Macau into the planning framework for the Pearl River Delta region. In the outline, it says that 'the state will encourage [Guangdong Province, Hong Kong, and Macau] to realize joint development of the cross-border logistics, convention and exhibition, cultural, and tourism industries; will heighten their mutual recognition of the professional qualifications for the banking, securities, insurance, appraisal, accounting, law, education, and medical service industries in order to create the conditions for developing service industries'.[5]

(3) Growing appeal of long-term assurance schemes

Long-term products, in particular those with an investment components, have been gaining popularity among policy-holders in recent years. Meanwhile, such products, commonly known as investment-linked assurance schemes (ILAS), have grown increasingly sophisticated and complex, befuddling many brokers and consumers.

In light of the financial tsunami of 2008, the OCI urged providers of ILAS products to be more equipped with financial knowledge in order to advise their clients properly. To that end, the agency introduced the Investment-linked Long Term Insurance Examination on 1 March 2010 for all those practitioners with less than seven years of documented experience in selling long-term products. In the same breath, insurers were advised to strengthen internal control over sales of long-term investment-linked products in order to minimize litigation risks.

(4) The rise of independent regulatory regime

In July 2010, the government's Financial Services and the Treasury Bureau unveiled a proposal to install an independent regulatory body to oversee the industry, thus following a well-established international practice. It is proposed that this new insurance authority, first considered in the mid-1990s, will replace the current, government-controlled Office of the Commissioner of Insurance.

The authority will be operationally independent from the government and financially self-sustaining. The proposed authority will have a staff of 237 people and an annual budget of $240 million, to be supported solely by licence fees paid by insurers and salespersons and a 0.1 % levy on insurance premiums paid by policyholders.

The authority, expected to be up and running by 2013 at the earliest, will licence all insurance brokers working for both banks and insurance firms but is empowered to preside over complaints and investigations only concerning insurance companies and their agents. The HKMA will have the power to investigate insurance complaints against the 18,000 bank-based brokers who sell about 30% of all insurance policies issued annually.

The new Insurance Authority will replace the current regime, which is to a large extent self-regulatory. At present, three non-statutory industry groups — the Hong Kong Federation of Insurers (HKFI), the Hong Kong Confederation of Insurance Brokers (HKCIB) and the Hong Kong Professional Insurance Brokers Association (HKPIBA) — are vested with limited investigatory and sanctioning powers. Government officials believed that this proposed regulatory body will help supervise this industry in a uniform, professional manner, while eliminating once and for all any appearance of conflict of interest.

In addition, the government proposed setting up a statutory appeals tribunal to handle appeals against decisions or penalties handed down by the Insurance Authority. An independent process review panel will be established to review internal operating procedures to ensure consistency and fairness as the new authority carries out its mandates.

The government solicited public comments on the proposal from July till October 2010 with plans to introduce the bill to establish the proposed regulatory body to the Legislative Council by 2011.

Clement Cheung
Commissioner of Insurance (2006–2009)
Hong Kong SAR

Over the past decade, Hong Kong's insurance industry has been growing steadily and rapidly providing career opportunities for many capable and aspiring professionals.

Globally, most multinational financial institutions now have business interests in many pies and so they face myriad risk factors in an increasingly complex investment environment. Take AIG, the global conglomerate, as an example. Its Asia-Pacific insurance operations have always been smooth sailing yet its U.S. holding company was nearly sunk by its investments in the sub-prime mortgage and credit derivative products.

For Hong Kong's insurers, the best, even-keeled strategy is to keep one eye on the global market and the other on the vast untapped mainland market.

Notes

Chapter 1

1. A. Chalkley. 1985. *Adventures and Perils: The First Hundred and Fifty Years of Union Insurance Society of Canton, Ltd*. Hong Kong: Ogilvy & Mather Public Relations (Asia) Ltd.
2. H. A. L. Cockrell, and E. Green. 1988. *The British Insurance Business: History and Archives*. Continuum International Publishing Group-Sheffie.
3. G. C. Allen, and A. G. Donnithorne. 1954. *Western Enterprise in Far Eastern Economic Development*. London: Allen & Unwin, p. 119.
4. M. Greenberg. 1998. *British Trade & the Opening of China 1800–1842*, p. 18.
5. E. Le Fevour. 1968. *Western Enterprise in Late Ch'ing China: A Selective Survey of Jardine, Matheson and Company's Operations 1842–1895*. Cambridge, Mass.: Harvard University Press, p. 136.
6. *North China Herald*, 26 November 1864, p. 191.
7. A decisive battle in the Greek War of Independence, in which the British, French, and Russian navies defeated Ottoman-Egyptian forces.
8. Lombard Insurance Group. 1986. *Lombard Insurance Group, 1836–1986*. Hong Kong: The Group, p. 15.
9. James Steuart. 1934. *Jardine, Matheson & Co. Afterwards Jardine, Matheson & Co. Limited: An Outline of the History of a China House for a Hundred Years 1832–1932*. London: The Westminster Press, pp. 36–37.
10. Chalkley, p. 5.
11. Chalkley, pp. 12–13.
12. Chalkley, p. 11.
13. Chalkley, p. 14.
14. Zhao Lanliang. 2003. *Research on the Contemporary Shanghai Insurance Market (1843–1937)*. Shanghai: Fudan University Press, p. 26.
15. S. C. Lockwood. 1971. *Augustine Heard and Company, 1858–1862: American Merchants in China*. Cambridge, Mass.: East Asian Research Center, Harvard University, pp. 106–108.

16. Zhao, p. 29.
17. Le Fevour, p. 136.
18. Lockwood, p. 107.
19. Le Fevour, p. 136.
20. The structure of Hong Kong Fire Insurance Co. was modelled on that of its British counterparts. In the early days in England the fire brigades were under the insurers' command; only later did the brigades fall under the police command. Even so, the insurers remained in close cooperation with the brigade and helped distribute educational material to raise awareness of precautionary measures against fires.
21. Zhao, p. 33.
22. Allen and Donnithorne, p. 120.
23. Steuart, pp. 36–37.
24. Fire Insurance Association of Hong Kong. 31 July 1987.
25. Lowe, Bingham, Matthews. 1962. *Notes on the History of the Firm as Secretaries of the Insurance Associations*.
26. Le Fevour, p. 21.
27. Le Fevour, p. 14.
28. Le Fevour, p. 24 footnote.
29. Le Fevour, p. 28.
30. *The Manufacturers Insurance Company, South China Hong Kong and Macau 1898–1976*, p. 1.

Chapter 2

1. J. Resnick, and R. Wong. 2000. *100 Years and Growing — The Story of Sincere*. Sincere Co. Ltd.
2. *Wing On Department Stores Celebrating 100 Years of Retailing*.

Chapter 3

1. Chalkley, p. 36.
2. Chalkley, p. 38.
3. Chalkley, p. 36.

4. Chalkley, p. 54.
5. Chalkley, p. 45.
6. Lombard Insurance Group. 1986. *Lombard Insurance Group, 1836–1986*. Hong Kong: The Group, p. 5.
7. R. Hutcheon. 1992. *A Burst of Crackers: The Li & Fung Story*. Hong Kong: Li & Fung Ltd. Press, p. 23.
8. The Accident & Marine Insurance Associations of Hong Kong. 17 August 1987.
9. C. A. Brook-Fox. 1982. *Marketing Effectiveness in the Hong Kong Insurance Industry*. Hong Kong: The University of Hong Kong. Unpublished MBA thesis, pp. 3–4.

Chapter 4

1. Y. C. Jao. 1984. 'The Financial Structure', in *The Business Environment in Hong Kong*, Oxford University Press, p. 170.
2. Jao, p. 170.
3. J. W. Matthews. 1964. *Insurance Markets of the World*. Swiss Reinsurance Company, p. 436.
4. P. Hugh. *Absolute Integrity: The Story of Royal Insurance 1845–1995*. Royal Insurance, p. 229.
5. C. A. Brook-Fox. 1982. *Marketing Effectiveness in the Hong Kong Insurance Industry*. Hong Kong, p. 4.
6. Brook-Fox. p. 5.
7. T. T. Yuen. 1986. *A Study on the Popularity of Utilizing Insurance Brokers by Industrial Concerns in Hong Kong for Management of Their Insurance Programme*. Hong Kong: The University of Hong Kong. Unpublished MBA thesis, pp. 4–5.
8. Yuen.
9. *Jardine, Matheson & Co Ltd: 150th Anniversary*. 1982. Hong Kong: The South China Morning Post.
10. Brook-Fox, p. 6.
11. *The Manufacturers Insurance Company, South China, Hong Kong and Macau 1898–1976*, p. 3.
12. The Hong Kong Export Credit Insurance Corp. 2006. *Forty Years of Development and Experience*, p. 45.
13. The Hong Kong Export Credit Insurance Corp. *Annual Report 1976–77*, p. 6.

Chapter 5

1. J. W. Matthews. 1964. *Insurance Market of the World, Swiss Reinsurance Company*, p. 436.
2. A. Hicks. 1983. Insurance Law Reform. *Law Lectures for Practitioners*. Hong Kong: Hong Kong Law Journal Ltd., p. 291.
3. Hicks, p. 284.
4. Hicks, p. 289.
5. Hong Kong Federation of Insurers. 1998. *The Story of the Hong Kong Federation of Insurers 1988–1998*. Hong Kong: Hong Kong Federation of Insurers, p. 18.
6. *The Story of the Hong Kong Federation of Insurers 1988–1998*, pp. 28, 25.

Chapter 6

1. Office of the Commissioner of Insurance. 2000. *Commemorating the 10th Anniversary, Office of the Commissioner of Insurance*. Hong Kong, p. 7.
2. The Law Reform Commission of Hong Kong. Press Release on Report on Laws on Insurance, 15 January 1986.
3. *Hong Kong Administrative Law Sourcebook's Hong Kong cases*. See http://law.hku.hk/hkadmlawsb/hkcases.htm
4. Insurance Companies Ordinance (Cap. 41).
5. Hong Kong Federation of Insurers. Press release on Life Insurance Council Announces Scheme to Protect Consumers, 28 September 1994.
6. Hong Kong Federation of Insurers. Press release on Life Insurance Council Offers Consumers Cooling-off Rights, 27 June 1996.
7. Hong Kong Federation of Insurers. Press release on Consumers Better Informed When Selecting Life Policies, 5 May 1998.
8. Office of the Commissioner of Insurance. *Hong Kong: An Ideal Captive Hub*. Web document. http://www.oci.gov.hk/framework/index08_01.html.
9. Office of the Commissioner of Insurance. 1997. *Hong Kong: An Ideal Domicile for Captives*.

Chapter 7

1. Office of the Commissioner of Insurance of Hong Kong SAR Government. 2000, p. 25.
2. KPMG, Reuters. 2005. *Foreign Insurers in China: Opportunity and Risk*. Hong Kong: KPMG & Reuters, p. 7.
3. KMPG, Reuters, p. 4.
4. The Hongkong & Shanghai Banking Corp. Press releases, http://www.pingan.com/about/en/news_70052.jsp#, May 2005.
5. KPMG Hong Kong's monthly insurance news summary: May 2005, http://www.kpmg.com.cn/en/virtual_library/Financial_services/insurance_notes/Insurancenotes0505.htm.

Conclusion

1. The Government of the Hong Kong Special Administrative Region. 2008. *Hong Kong Annual Report and Hong Kong Annual Digest of Statistics*.
2. V. Fung. 'Supply Chain Orchestration: Its Concepts and Relevance to the Insurance Industry'. *Hong Kong Chamber of Insurance Intermediaries 2007 Yearbook*, p. 18.
3. Census and Statistics Department, Hong Kong Government. 2002. *Thematic Household Survey Report No. 9*, p. 65.
4. Census and Statistics Department, Hong Kong Government. 2002. *Thematic Household Survey Report No. 9*, p. 65.
5. National Development and Reform Commission. 2009. *Outline of the Plan for the Reform and Development of the Pearl River Delta (2008–2020).*

Index